# Digital
# Sub-editing
## and Design

**Stephen Quinn**

Focal Press

OXFORD  AMSTERDAM  BOSTON  LONDON    NEW YORK    PARIS
SAN DIEGO  SAN FRANCISCO  SINGAPORE  SYDNEY  TOKYO

Focal Press
An imprint of Elsevier Science
Linacre House, Jordan Hill, Oxford OX2 8DP
225 Wildwood Avenue, Woburn, MA 01801-2041

First published 2001
Reprinted 2002

**British Library Cataloguing in Publication Data**
A catalogue record for this book is available from the British Library

**Library of Congress Cataloguing in Publication Data**
A catalogue record for this book is available from the Library of Congress

ISBN 0 240 51639 7

For information on all Focal Press publications visit
our website at www.focalpress.com

Designer: Stephen Quinn

Printed and bound in Great Britain

# Contents

## SECTION A: ELECTRONIC EDITING

## SECTION B: DIGITAL DESIGN

## SECTION C: NEW MEDIA

# Acknowledgements

My major thanks go to my wife, Deirdre Quinn-Allan, for giving me the time to complete the manuscript. She selflessly took care of our daughter Tobi and our son Felix to allow me time to write. Deirdre, thank you for your patience, tolerance and love.

Thanks also to my former and current journalism students, who all served as guinea pigs for some of the ideas outlined here, and to the working editors who contributed their expertise and help. In particular I'd like to thank Bruce Kaplan and Clive Dorman at *The Age* in Australia, and Debbie Wolfe at the *St Petersburg Times* in Florida. Thanks also to my colleagues at Deakin University: Gail Sedorkin, Lyndsay Sharp, John Lawrence and John Tidey.

# Introduction

REVELATION is too strong a word for what happened, but it is fair to say that this book began with a mini insight. In 1996 I was doing a casual editing shift on a regional daily newspaper. Having been away from Australia for more than a decade, I was keen to re-acquaint myself with how Australian newspapers worked. Perhaps it was the instant coffee, or maybe I was just feeling relaxed after the meal break, but in one of the few quiet moments that evening my mind slipped back to when I first encountered the world of the sub-editor. No longer was I sitting behind a Cybergraphic computer terminal; I had been transported back to the kidney-shaped table around which sat the sub-editors at the *Newcastle Morning Herald* in New South Wales, Australia, 20 years earlier.

The business of subbing, I realized, had changed significantly in the past two decades. Gone were the paste pots, razor blades, pencils and manual typewriters we used to assemble and mark up copy. Gone were the fierce-looking nails set in heavy lead bases on which we 'spiked' unnecessary copy. Gone also were the type booklets we used to calculate characters when trying to fit a headline. Cadets no longer trailed streamers of paper as they rushed about delivering proof pages. Men in green eye-shades no longer hunched over a jumble of paper, assembling stories from teleprinter print-outs and reporters' copy. A bank of teleprinters no longer chattered in the background, pouring out streams of copy from domestic and international news agencies. Now everything was digital, or about to become so.

It has taken a few years since 1996 to get these ideas into print, but the simple fact is that the digital revolution has changed sub-editing radically. The role of the sub-editor or copy editor is also changing. In the UK, South Africa, Hong Kong, Canada, Australia and New Zealand practitioners are dubbed subs; in the US they are called copy editors. People entering the business will need to embrace computers enthusiastically if they want to do the job properly. The main message of this book is **prepare for change**, because it is upon us and causing upheavals, if not creating a revolution. Change will continue to be part of life for information age journalists.

**W**e have all heard the marketers' spiels about the 'paperless office'. Like many of the myths associated with computers, that proved to be a nonsense. It is almost as silly as the notion popularized in the mid 1980s that people would soon have too much leisure time and would need help organizing their lifestyles. Compared with the mid 1970s, the subs' room of the new century contains about the same amount of paper, though the quantity of information that arrives in the news room has risen markedly. It is worth going back 20 years or so to revisit newspapers and magazines where journalists assembled their publications using 'copy' paper and other tools that had been around for hundreds of years.

Copy paper consisted of pieces of clean newsprint cut into A5 rectangles. Reporters typed stories on three layers with carbons sandwiched between them, numbering each page and giving it a 'slug' to identify the story. The term slug came from the days when each story was given a unique name — usually one or two words. Thus the first page of a story about a storm would be slugged 'storm 1' and subsequent pages would be called 'storm 2', 'storm 3' and so on. When the story was set in type, a piece of type with that name — known as a slug — was assigned to the proofs (for more details see page 74). Subs also used copy paper for writing headlines and captions. We calculated headlines by consulting type booklets to find out how many characters we had to play with over the allocated width. Then it was a case of playing with words to find a head that fitted and still made sense. All that seems a long time ago.

Now everything in what is called the production process — the assembly of pages after reporters have submitted their stories — is done on computers. These tools have produced massive changes in newspapers and magazines. In some respects they make the job easier, but they also place more responsibility on the subs' shoulders. This book specifically concerns itself with the **changing role of the editor** in the digital era. For the sake of variety, the terms 'sub' and 'editor' are used interchangeably. Each chapter covers specific skills that an editor has traditionally needed, and also considers the new opportunities and responsibilities that technology makes possible. The result is a combination of talents that are most appropriate for subs in the digital age.

**V**ery few reporters, I am sure, plan to become subs when they enter journalism. While many journalism courses offer one subject or unit in subbing as part of the undergraduate major or degree, few (if any) teach subbing as a specific qualification. Most people graduate from journalism programmes looking to work as reporters. Traditionally, most subs have entered the profession after a stint as a reporter (though that is changing). Subbing still seems to be something that reporters wander into because they think it will help their writing (it does) or because their boss needs more hands on deck on the subs' table.

Why would anyone give up the relative glamour of the by-line and expense account to sit around a table processing other people's words? That question has always intrigued me. Perhaps people become subs because they tire of chasing fire engines and the odd hours associated with a reporter's life. Reporting the same endless council meetings and football matches does lose its attraction after a while. Subs tell me it is nice to have regular hours — even if subbing on a morning paper involves starting anywhere between 4pm and 6pm and working until midnight or 2am the next morning. Perhaps it is the sort of job people enter out of curiosity. As a junior reporter I wondered who those strange people were huddled around that table at the other end of the building. When school groups visited the newspaper, some of the subs would don green plastic eye-shades and those old-fashioned arm suspenders used to protect shirtsleeves from ink. The subs thought it was funny and would put on a performance for the school children, chewing pensively on pencils or mumbling about the copy in front of them. Perhaps they wanted to maintain the mystique of the subs' table.

One of the delights of working on a good subs' table is the sense of camaraderie that it engenders. That has always been an attraction of the job — the chance to spend time with the talented and literate individuals who work as sub-editors. In the introductory journalism text *Kiwi Journalist*, Mike Paterson pronounced in a chapter on sub-editing that one privilege of being a reporter was the opportunity 'to breath the same air as sub-editors' (1992: 184).

Skill with words remains a prerequisite for working as a sub. In many countries, production experience is vital for promotion to senior editorial positions. Henry Wickham Steed, editor of *The Times* between 1919 and 1922, said that of the members of a newspaper staff he was 'inclined to give first place to the sub-editors as a body'. In its publication the *Newspaper Subediting Bible*, the National Council for the Training of Journalists in England listed sub-editing as 'one of the great specialisations in journalism', noting that the sub-editor who was good at his or her job was 'perhaps the nearest thing to what might be described as the complete journalist' (1982: 2). Yet choosing to be a sub means choosing a relatively anonymous role. It is rare to find a newspaper that includes a byline for the sub who takes a mediocre story and makes it memorable. Incidentally, at least one American daily, the *Gazette Telegraph* in Colorado Springs, has been experimenting with giving copy-editors a byline for writing the headline and editing the text.

The public seems to appreciate little of the sub's role even though, as you will discover in the chapters on design and picture editing, the sub has a major role in influencing what people read. Journalism students are often surprised to hear that reporters seldom if ever write headlines. Subs are the anonymous people who put newspapers, magazines (and also broadcast news programmes) together. After 20 years on and off as a sub, I do not have an answer. By now we could probably be forgiven for forgetting the question. Perhaps there is a certain satisfaction in knowing that we are one of the key people in the production process. Perhaps it is the delight to be found in writing a good caption, or the joy of crafting a witty headline that fits. Perhaps it is the cruel glee felt when correcting, and chuckling over, the appalling grammar of a so-called celebrity 'writer'.

# How to use this book

Sub-editing has long been considered a craft that sometimes rises to the level of art. Meanwhile, reporters are described as writers, seemingly a far more honourable profession. It is time to move beyond that misapprehension. This book is about the art and craft of subbing in the information age, but it is also an appeal to its practitioners to realize they are members of a unique profession.

A special skill like sub-editing cannot be taught entirely out of a book. But this book can be used as a mentor. It can be particularly effective if combined with guidance from an experienced sub. If that is not possible, regard this book as an old hand sitting next to you and offering the occasional useful advice..I began this book by asking myself what would I need and want to know if I were starting as a sub. The answers are reflected in the structure of this book.

It also important here to remember the context in which we find the changing profession of journalism. In some ways, the changing role of the sub reflects the changing role of journalism in the information age. One of the biggest issues is information overload. In his book *Data Smog: Surviving the Information Glut*, David Shenk maintains that information has become superabundant in the past 50 years.

In an information-glutted world, journalists are more necessary than ever. 'In a world with vastly more information than it can process, journalists are the most important processors we have,' Shenk says. Given that subs sit at the centre of the production process, they can dominate and influence this synthesizing role — summarizing for readers what is important, and discarding the rest.

Meanwhile, print publications must accept that broadcasters and the Internet deliver most of the freshest news — 'what' has happened. Because of the time involved in printing and delivering publications, newspapers and magazines will always lag behind those other news outlets. Newspapers and magazines need to adjust their role, to become the primary source of the 'how' and 'why' of news. This will be another prevailing theme.

# Structure of the book

Most subs start as copy editors, in the sense that they are expected to process body text and write headlines and captions before they are allowed to design pages. The first section concentrates on editing in the electronic age. This section is designed to give you the tools to be able to edit effectively. It shows how to write powerful headlines and captions, and how to edit body text quickly and cleanly. **Chapter 1** considers the editor's changing role in the digital environment and briefly gives an overview of the production process. **Chapter 2** introduces the tools of the trade for the sub and shows how to produce clear and concise text. **Chapter 3** provides a step-by-step process for writing great headlines. **Chapter 4** does the same for writing effective captions.

The next section concentrates on design in the digital environment. **Chapter 5** introduces new subs to the arcane world of typography and the related issues of readability and legibility because typography is the foundation for all design. **Chapter 6** covers design principles, and how these principles can be applied to print and electronic publications. **Chapter 7** looks at the skills of picture editing — image choice and cropping — and touches on the ethical issues related to image selection and manipulation. **Chapter 8** investigates other forms of visual presentation such as illustrations, info-graphics and other visual aids, and sees them as ways to help readers deal with a scourge of new millennium life, information overload.

The final section applies these skills and methods to the world of new media and the World Wide Web. **Chapter 9** recognizes that on the Web, text is possibly more important than image. It considers recent research into how people look at and navigate Web pages, and applies the research to that medium. **Chapter 10** looks at how print design principles can (and cannot) be applied to Web pages.

Each chapter begins with an overview and ends with exercises and a list of references and/or recommended reading. So what are you waiting for? Turn to Chapter 1 to find out about the changing role of the sub-editor in the digital world, and the skills that you need to hone or acquire. Enjoy.

# References

Andrews, Allan (2000). 'Dumbing down the Press: The disappearing copy editor' in *The American Reporter,* 1 June 2000 <www.american-reporter.com>.

Hodgson, F.W. (1993). *Subediting: A handbook of modern newspaper editing and production.* Oxford: Focal Press.

National Council for the Training of Journalists (1982). *Newspaper Subediting Bible.* London: NCTJ.

Paterson, Mike (1992). Chapter 25 'The role of subeditors' in Tucker's *Kiwi Journalist.* Auckland: Longman Paul.

Provis, Michael (1996). *Editing Australian Newspapers.*
    Geelong: Deakin University Press.

Shenk, David (1997). *Data Smog: Surviving the Information
    Glut.* Harper Edge: San Francisco.

# 1 The editor's changing yet consistent role

## Summary

- Changing work practices
- Key people in production
- Two eras of digital editing
- The sub's role
- Skills a sub should have
- Tools of the trade
- The flow of news
- Main editorial conferences

THE title of this chapter may seem a contradiction but it is not. The editor's role is changing because of digital technology, but in many respects the skills and processes remain the same. Some of the changes have come about because of editors' expanded roles — they do more because they are also proof readers and compositors — and the fact that they need to have highly-tuned technical abilities. The skills remain unchanged. They are simply being re-applied in the digital domain. The processes discussed in this book reflect this. For example, the skill of writing a great headline is still highly prized on an editors' table, and it has always been thus. Technology both hinders and helps the process — we can kern a head to fit but in untrained hands, this squeezing of type can distort the appearance and design of a page.

Academic Dr Rosslyn Reed believes that the introduction of cold metal technology in the early 1980s significantly affected the sub-editors' job. Increased responsibility for the final product, formerly shared with compositors and proof readers, increased stress and job dissatisfaction. At the same time, technology simplified reporters' jobs, in some respects making that a more attractive option. Developments in pagination in the 1990s extended subs' tasks and responsibilities. With pagination, subs were 'responsible for all pre-press newspaper production up to the plate-making stage'. Reed also noted a shift in ownership to 'corporate and international' groups, which made news organisations 'more structured, formalized and bureaucratized'. Sophisticated production technologies, she said, were 'further transforming old workplace cultures and management practices'.

# Changing work practices

Another academic, Jackie Ewart, noted that pagination systems had introduced a new approach to editing in many news rooms. Editors undertake one or more of three roles: layout, design or copy editing. 'Layout sub-editors, usually the chief layout sub, work with the newspaper's art director in drawing up layouts. Design sub-editors place copy, [and] handle photographs and graphics. Copy sub-editors check spelling, grammar and the arrangement of a story, and copy fit . . . Design sub-editors are responsible for the overall appearance of the newspaper, while copy sub-editors look after content and style.' The two groups, she noted, 'have minimal contact with each other'. It remains to be seen whether this Fordist approach produces better papers.

Perhaps one of the biggest changes relates to the fact that the media are more noticeably a business than, say, 20 years ago. Marketing has emerged as a major factor in the selling of publications to an external audience. Think of headlines and other display elements as another form of marketing, this time for an internal audience. Their job is to 'sell' stories as well as entice people to read. In a congested market place, and in an environment marked by economic rationalism, the need to promote a publication becomes paramount. This means that subs need to know their market and their audience.

When considered as a business, daily newspapers are unique in the sense that the 'live' sections are built almost from scratch each day. No other industry encompasses such a short span between starting a product and producing it. An ocean liner takes years to build; it may be months before a petrol station is operating. But the news, sport and business pages of a daily newspaper are put together in a few hours. News subs are consequently up against the clock. Allan Andrews, writing in the *American Reporter* <www.american-reporter.com>, believes that American newspapers have been leaning towards a broadcast model in terms of structure and staffing, with a resulting diminution of the role of the copy editor. Another consequence, he believes, is that newspapers have 'drastically diminished the linguistic skill demands on the copyeditor'. We shall discuss this later.

# Key people in production

Who are the key people in this construction process? The public thinks it is reporters because their bylines appear each day. While important, reporters are not the key people. Subs are. *The Age*, for example, could be produced without local reporters, using copy from news agencies such as Australian Associated Press and Reuters. This has happened during strikes, and digital technology makes that process relatively easy for managers required by their contracts to work through strikes. But those managers work damn hard during any strike because of the volume of copy they process, and they work as subs not reporters. Overall, the production team — generally all subs and promoted sub-editors — are the vital people in the editorial process. What skills do these people need, and have they changed with time? The sub's role in producing all forms of publications has changed significantly in the past two decades, because of the influence of technology. In fact, technology has been a consistent catalyst in affecting and changing editorial work practices for more than two centuries. The introduction of steam-driven printing presses in the mid nineteenth century, for example, increased the number of papers that could be produced and led to mass-market papers. Headlines started to appear near the end of the nineteenth century, though they were very different to the heads we see in twenty-first century papers. Just over a hundred years ago, headlines were set in layers and they effectively told the whole story. Figure 1.1 shows an example of the headline style common at the start of century in *The Age* of 3 May 1915. Headlines told the story in a series of vertical decks.

**Figure 1.1: The front page of The Age of 3 May 1915. Note the headline style of telling the story in vertical decks. The lead tells of the landing of Australian troops at Gallipoli in World War I.**

Rationing of paper during both world wars meant that newspapers had to be more tightly edited. Despite the increased volume of news that war generated, proprietors were forced to cut the size of newspapers because of the high price of newsprint. One consequence was a drive for better edited and more concisely written newspapers. In his book *The Press in Australia,* Henry Mayer quoted a memo from Sir Keith Murdoch (father of Rupert) to his staff during World War I: 'Always the need will be for condensation — all the news pointed, clear, terse — never an unnecessary word'. War forced papers to be 'more pithily written' and brought the sub-editor's role to the fore. Mayer cited five factors that he said shaped the news in the first half of the twentieth century. The main one was the introduction of headlines as we know them. The others included expanded news sources, increased communication costs, accelerated news distribution and the subjectivity of news values.

# Two eras of digital editing

Debbie Wolfe, training editor for the *St Petersburg Times* in the United States, believes there have been two main eras of 'digital editing'. One was the 'non-manual typewriter' period using video display terminals or personal computers. The other was the pagination era that combines digital editing with digital layout. 'The newspaper industry in the United States is undergoing tremendous change right now with the pagination era.' But she believes that the biggest change has not involved the mechanics of switching technologies — rather it has been dealing with the 'people factor': 'The resistance to change in general: anxiety, fear of losing one's job or not being able to "make it" as the job has been redefined.'

Wolfe maintains there are strong parallels with the radical changes that industry and society went through from the 'farming era' to the 'industrial era' and on to the 'information era'. This should be the framework for any study of changing work practices for editors, she says.

In effect then, subbing falls into two types of job. One is technical and production oriented, in the sense that the sub has to process copy in an almost mechanical way. The other role is much more creative: writing good headlines and captions is one of the great literary skills. And producing

interesting page layouts is yet another creative act. To understand these, we need to digress briefly to consider how the
human brain works. How does brain function relate to subbing, you ask? Relax. All will be revealed soon.

Psycho-biologist Roger Sperry received the Nobel Prize for
Medicine in 1981 for discovering that the two hemispheres in
the human brain have specialized functions. That is, the right
and left hemispheres perform different tasks. Put simply, the
left works best with words, numbers, mathematics, logic and
linear sequence. The right deals best with pictures, patterns,
rhythm, imagination and spatial matters. Since then, think-
ers such as Tony Buzan have concluded that creativity is a
whole-brain function. When people use both hemispheres, the
*corpus callosum* (the bundle of nerve fibres, three to five
millimetres in width, that connects the hemispheres) hums
with activity. When people perform a mainly left-hemisphere
activity, such as editing text, the *corpus callosum* is silent.
Similarly, when people mainly use their right hemisphere, the
*corpus callosum* is quiet.

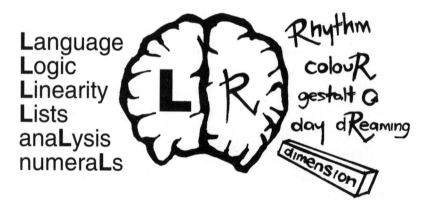

**Figure 1.2: The different functions of the two hemispheres.**

When this knowledge is related to editing, we sometimes
need to use one hemisphere exclusively, and at other times we
need the other. For example, proof reading relies almost
entirely on the skills of the left hemisphere with its ability to
focus on detail. But to create, we need to integrate the hemi-

spheres. Figure 1.2 shows the different roles of the brain's hemispheres.

It is vital to remain relaxed, because tension kills creativity. How do we remain relaxed while competing against the clock? Surely this generates tension? People have discovered various ways, such as deep breathing or going for a short walk or taking our mind off a task that hinders us (and letting our subconscious work on the problem while we are doing something else). Using artificial ways to relax or distract our minds, such as mind-altering chemicals, is not recommended, though it often helps at the end of the day's work when we need to wind down.

# The sub's role

Let us look, then, at the editor's main role. The first section of this chapter considers that role. The next two sections look at a sub's tools of the trade and the general flow of news and how that flow affects the sub's job. In his excellent book *The Simple Subs Book*, Leslie Sellers maintains that subs are 'in the polishing business'. Their job, he believes, is to improve the raw product. 'It is in the big, highly-tuned newspapers that the craft of subbing is developed to the highest degree.' Though published in 1972, the book remains an excellent resource for novice and expert editors.

In a nutshell, subs have five main roles. They need to:

1. ensure the stories they edit are easy to understand
2. check everything that can be checked, and check again
3. ensure that writers are not leading the newspaper into trouble with the law
4. process stories against technical and production requirements such as ensuring copy is in house style, and cutting or expanding the story to fit the news hole
5. create headlines, captions and design pages

# Skills a sub should have

What sort of skills or talents should a sub have? Sellers admits that it is rare to find one sub with all the skills. Some are 'utterly reliable when it comes to cutting a specialist's story by half, who sub to exact length, who never bust headlines' while others who can write sparkling captions or headlines 'may well make the most disastrous errors of judgement on length'. These differences of temperament can improve any paper, if properly used, he says. Certainly technology takes the pain out of fitting copy. In some respects, the differences reflect the two sides of the brain that Sperry identified.

On papers with relatively few subs, the 'all-rounder' becomes a vital member of the staff. Sellers' book concentrates on developing the all-rounder, as does this one. Let us consider the skills an ideal sub should have. They should:

■ know their audience (because this influences tone)

■ know the English language intimately

■ know how to use a range of reference books

■ be numerate

■ respect the writer's work

■ know the law, or who to turn to

■ know the house style

■ understand typography and design principles.

Editors need to know their audience because this knowledge will directly influence the type of publication they produce. They must have an excellent grasp of English, and also the humility to admit their ignorance (in the true sense of the word, meaning lacking in knowledge) and consult a reference book. Editors must also be numerate, or know how to check numerical data such as surveys, statistics and the like.

They must also respect the work of the writer they are editing. In other words, only bad editors change for the sake of changing. Unnecessary editing destroys a writer's morale and, perhaps worse, uses valuable time that could be spent creating headlines or captions. Editors must also know enough about the laws affecting the media to be able to recognize potential problems. Editors do not need to be experts in defamation. But they must be able to sniff it out, so they can refer the problem to an editorial executive.

Editors tend to be guardians of a publication's style, so they need to know where to go to check that something conforms to house style. With most production (front-end) systems, the technology usually allows that style to be stored in an accessible format — often on an intranet or some form of Web-based file. Finally, a good sub needs to have a reasonable grasp of typography and design principles. The former is the foundation stone of good design. Subs need to know that some type faces cannot be squeezed or altered too much. Publication design is an art form that merges with craft. A well-constructed page is aesthetically pleasing, makes it easy for people to absorb information, yet contains as much information as possible without appearing crowded.

A sub's skills come from his or her background and education. No *one* attribute makes a good sub. The best subs have many skills and attributes. These skills and attributes may come from wide reading, from having travelled extensively and from having done a variety of jobs. They come from an insatiable curiosity about how things work. They come from a thorough knowledge of grammar and spelling. A good sub has a broad general knowledge. A good sub has a sense of humour. A good sub knows how to check facts. A good sub can write a catchy headline that fits. A good sub understands typography and the principles of publication design. A good sub knows how to cut the fat out of copy and make it fit an allocated space. A good sub understands the laws of defamation and contempt of court. A good sub can write a witty caption. A good sub knows a publication's style and how to apply it. A good sub . . . the list goes on!

Not every sub will have every skill. As any racing tyro knows, it is a case of horses for courses. This book provides an overview of most of the skills but there is always room for improvement. This book works on the principle that the skills outlined above can be taught, provided the trainee *actually does the job*. Mastery comes from doing the job combined with appropriate feedback. The more a person works as a sub, the more they learn and the better sub they become — provided any errors are corrected. Each story you sub and each headline you write is reference material for the next story you edit. With time you will surprise yourself with the amount of information you acquire. Welcome to one of the most fascinating and challenging jobs in the media.

---

**You can remember the sub-editor's role by thinking of these Cs:**
■ **Correcting (grammar, spelling and house style)**
■ **Condensing**
■ **Clarifying**
■ **Cutting (or expanding)**
■ **Checking**
■ **Creating compelling intros, captions and headlines**

---

# Tools of the trade

We move now onto the tools of the editor's trade. Sub-editors have few apparent tools, in the sense that dentists or mechanics have tools. Subs cannot produce a collection of drills or spanners from a tray or kit bag. Many of a sub's skills are internalized — based on experience and intuition. Ask a sub why she chose to change an introduction or corrected the grammar in a story, and often she will be unable to explain the process — she just knew it had to be done. And those changes will be appropriate for the publication.

In a sense, the changes will be the product of years of working with one primary tool — words. A mechanic's spanners or a dentist's drills are vital for their trade. Not so for subs. When time is short, as it often is, they must rely on their internalized skills. What is this intuition that leads them to make changes to copy? Where does it come from? Some of it comes from several years' experience as a reporter — an excellent reason why newspapers should continue to insist that a sub has been a reporter for at least two to three years. Some senior subs say they 'sense' a problem. One old hand said he knows something is wrong when the 'hackles rise on the back of my neck'. Another said: 'It's like a twang in my mind — something tells me that something's not right.' It boils down to instinct, they say.

Having said that, subs still need some experience of the world (this generates a good general knowledge) and a thorough knowledge of good English. You cannot explain problems to a writer whose work you are editing without a knowledge of the tools of the trade — the English language. This is fine for someone who has been doing the job for years, but what about the novice? You need to find a mentor.

> **Mastery comes from doing the job, combined with appropriate feedback.**

## Find a mentor

This book is designed to provide some guidelines and ground rules for good subbing practice. It is intended for the novice. It could be seen as a substitute for the 'old hand' sitting next to the newcomer, but in the best of all possible worlds the two processes work best together. It helps to have an experienced sub around for advice. That is why I recommend a mentor system, where the new sub spends some time at the elbow of an experienced hand. And they must do the job on the job. Doing is still the best way to learn.

# The flow of news

This final section covers the daily flow of news and how it is handled. Reporters probably have little to do with their paper's daily schedule. But the sub is less involved with a particular report and more concerned with the paper's overall content. This generalization applies more when you start doing some of the more senior subbing tasks such as revise sub or chief sub. The revise (or check) sub double checks every edited story. Often they do their checking on page proofs. As part of their job they note clashes in headlines next to each other. You can stay on the revise sub's good side by ensuring that everything you send them has been checked and double checked. The chief sub is the most senior editor on the desk. Often she or he is the last person to see a page before it is printed. On small publications, the chief sub and perhaps one other will design all pages. On big papers, the chief sub may design the main news pages. Other sections such as business and sport have their own chief sub and subs.

# Main editorial conferences

This section considers what is involved in producing a daily paper — in this case a morning publication. If you work on an evening or a Sunday, you will need to make the appropriate time adjustments. The aim is to provide an overview of typical daily events. All times are approximate. Reporters on morning papers work various shifts: 9am–5pm, or 10am–6pm, or noon–8pm, or 1pm–9pm, or perhaps 3pm–11pm. For evening meetings or events, for example, they will be rostered to start and finish late.

On a major capital city paper like *The Age* in Australia, the main editorial conference starts at 10am. The chief of staff or news editor or city editor (titles vary from country to country) will distribute a preliminary list based on what various departments have supplied. The contents of a newspaper are fluid and the assignments list seldom represents what appears next day. Interestingly, digital tools have generally not meant that papers are produced later. If anything, fewer staff and more pages mean that the deadline for the front page of a major daily paper can be as early as 9.30pm, and in some cases earlier (8.30pm) for extra large papers such as weekend editions. Late morning or about lunchtime a paper's editorial or leader writers meet the editor and other senior staff members to discuss the editorials. The senior sub-editor who is responsible for the editorial page usually attends the meeting. She or he might be called on to make suggestions about possible topics for leaders. The night editor and the news editor arrive in the early afternoon and begin sifting through copy that has already arrived from agencies and early reporters. The chief of staff liaises with the day news editor and they work together during the day to develop the preliminary news list. This list is deliberately flexible because anything can happen in the hours before the deadline for the first edition. The news chief sub-editor and the other subs arrive at varying times, depending on the pages for which they are responsible. News subs start about 3pm or 4pm and work until about 10pm or 11pm. Others start as late as 6pm and finish about 2am next day.

Subs in departments other than news start earlier. A features sub will often work day hours, or begin at 11am or noon. Staggered hours allow time for early pages to be subbed, designed and sent to the production room in the afternoon, or often a couple of days before. It is the only way to process a lot of copy — it would be impossible to write, design and sub a 96-page paper overnight. This method allows subs more time to work on 'live' news pages — usually the front few pages of the news, sports and business sections.

## Main news conference

The main news conference starts about 6pm. This is where departmental heads negotiate for space. Space is dictated by the advertising that has already been sold. The day of the week and newsworthy events also influence who gets what space. For example, Sunday's and Monday's papers usually have extra pages allocated for sports results from the weekend.

With major international events such as the Olympics or a war, the number of pages for foreign news would be increased. Department heads present their lists to the main news conference. Those who attend include the editor or his deputy, the night editor, the news editor, the night editor, the business editor, the foreign editor and the sports editor. Afterwards, the editorial executives return to read the copy that has arrived during the afternoon meetings. The news editor, associate or deputy news editors and night editor decide which stories will be given prominence and where the stories will be placed. The copy is then released to the subs to be processed.

What decides what is a 'good story'? News selection is like standing on shifting sand but editorial executives maintain that several factors influence the choice. If a story is exclusive or original it has a good chance of being published. An 'exclusive' is an important story that no other paper has. The quality of the writing and the reporter's initiative also influence selection. Time is another factor — often a later story will supersede a good earlier story because of the time each arrives and the time each happened. Some papers like to include late-breaking stories and reports that throw forward to that day to ensure the front page remains 'fresh'.

A paper's 'tone' is another factor. Papers of record like *The Guardian* in the UK or *The New York Times* tend to run more political and economic stories compared with tabloid publications that include more human interest stories. The quality of the photograph or illustration with a story also influences whether that story appears in print and where. News executives emphasize the 'organic nature' of news, suggesting that assessment of a story's worth tends to be subjective and the result of many factors.

The final news conference is held about 9.30pm, and really only concerns itself with updates for the main news pages. For that reason it is relatively brief. The news editor and his or her associates need to get away to work on the active news pages. Subs often have only three to four hours to process copy for the first edition, depending on when that copy arrives.

The next chapter considers the main ingredients that subs have to work with as they create each day's 'live' news pages — words. A glossary of subbing terms is available at the end of this book.

# Exercises

1. Observing the subs' desk at your local newspaper. Write a 400-word report on your observations.

2. If you are new to editing, ask a sub to describe their job to you. Discuss what you learned with a friend or colleague.

3. Subscribe to two types of newspapers — a paper of record and a tabloid that specializes in entertainment, for example. Compare them. Note how they treat the same event differently, and how the headlines and choice of words varies. Write a 500-word article about your findings.

# References

Bowles, Dorothy & Borden, Diane (2000). *Creative Editing.* Third edition. Stamford, CT: Wadsworth.

Buzan, Tony (1972). *Use your head.* London: BBC Books.

Ewart, Jacqui (1999). 'Design dominates sub-editing' in *Australian Journalism Review*, vol. 21(3), 93–112.

Hodgson, F.W. (1993). *Subediting: A handbook of modern newspaper editing and production.* Oxford: Focal Press.

Hodgson, F.W. (1998). *New Subediting: Apple-Mac, Quark XPress and After.* Oxford: Focal Press.

Kaplan, Bruce (2000). *Editing Made Easy: Secrets of the professionals.* Second edition. Sandringham, Australia.

Mayer, Henry (1968). *The Press in Australia.* Melbourne: Lansdowne Press.

Quinn, Stephen (1999). *The art of learning.* Geelong: Deakin University Press.

Reed, Rosslyn (1999). 'Celebrities and "soft options": Engendering print journalism in the era of hi-tech' in *Australian Journalism Review*, vol. 21(3), 81–92.

Sellers, Leslie (1972). *The Simple Subs Book.* Oxford: Pergamon Press.

# 2 Words, glorious words: Editing body text

## Summary
- The basic parts of speech
- Advice from Mark Twain
- The essence of editing
- Sentence types
- The basic principles of editing
- Lessons from the *Bible*

THE skill of producing clear yet concise body text can be likened to playing with Lego blocks. My son enjoys playing with those coloured plastic blocks because, he says, you can do 'cool things' with them. Those simple blocks can be fashioned into a vast range of interesting shapes. So it is with the English language. But instead of Lego blocks we have words. They can be fashioned into sentences and paragraphs, which become news stories and feature articles. But unlike Lego blocks, you need to understand how to use words. That is probably the most essential skill a sub needs.

To understand our language, you need to appreciate the concepts of grammar and syntax. Grammar is the set of rules and conventions that form the basis of our language. Syntax is the orderly arrangement of words in their most appropriate form. Early English grammars were based on Latin, which was overly rigid. English still has rules but they are not absolute. For example, nowhere in English grammar will you find rules that forbid you to split an infinitive, end a sentence with a preposition, or start with a conjunction. These are matters of style, and you should refer to your publication's style book for clarification.

A writer ignorant of the rules of grammar and syntax faces major disadvantages. A sub who does not know them is a liability. So we begin this chapter with an introduction to the basic parts of speech and then move on to how these Lego blocks can best be combined.

# The basic parts of speech

English has eight parts of speech. They are the noun, pronoun, adjective, verb, adverb, preposition, conjunction and interjection. You need to understand them because they are your tools. It is possible to communicate without understanding them, but you cannot communicate with precision. Just as you would have difficulty helping a mechanic repair an engine if you did not know the difference between a spanner and a screwdriver. Similarly, a surgeon cannot communicate with precision to an assistant if neither understands the tools to which each refers. 'Pass me that sharp thingy, would you please nurse, you know — the one with the long handle . . .'.

As a sub you will need to explain to reporters why you changed a problem with copy. This job becomes significantly easier if you have the right tools. In other words, you need to know the basic parts of speech. If you are not sure, refer to Appendix 1 for a primer (pages 165–170).

## An important rule

English can best be described as a language of conventions rather than rules. But one basic and important rule of

English says that the verb must agree with the subject in person and number. It is never the other way around. This is a simple rule but too often it is forgotten. Thus you would write:

**Spelling is important.** (Because 'spelling' is a singular subject. Revision for finding the subject: Ask yourself who or what is important.)

But: **Spelling and grammar are important.** (Because the subject here is 'spelling and grammar' and it is plural.)

Note that there are some exceptions. Appendix 1 contains details. It is worthwhile here to review the basic sentence structure used in journalism. It can be expressed thus:

**Subject + verb + object (also known as predicate)**

This form is the basis of the simple sentence (see later in this chapter). It is clear and easy to understand. Placing the subject at the start of a sentence forces the reporter or narrator to write or speak in the active voice. It is also more natural, in the sense that it imitates the way we speak. And it saves words because its opposite, known as passive voice, uses more words. Here is an example of a simple sentence in the active voice:

**The rat (subject) ate (verb) the cheese (object).**

The passive version would be:

**The cheese (object) was eaten (verb) by the rat (subject).**

Note that the passive requires more words and is more complicated. It also sounds wrong to your inner ear, unless like legal executives you have been trained to write this way.

## How to locate the subject

Nouns and pronouns can be the subject or the object of a sentence, depending on their position and the way the sentence is constructed. How do you identify the subject and the object? Easy: Question the verb. Ask who or what is doing the action of the verb (in this case, who is eating?). Answer: The rat. Therefore the rat is the subject. To find the object, ask who or what is having the action done to it — in this case who or what is being eaten? Answer: The cheese. The cheese is the object. Another way to find the object is to ask who or what is receiving the action of the verb.

The process also applies for active and passive voice, and when pronouns replace nouns such as in this example:

**It (subject) ate (verb) the cheese (object).**

In this situation, the pronoun replaces the noun, but is still the subject.

## Care with adjectives and adverbs

An adjective describes or modifies a noun or a pronoun. And an adverb describes or modifies a verb, adjective or another adverb. Think of the 'ad' in adjective and adverb as a way of remembering this concept — the adjective 'adds' to the noun and the adverb 'adds' to the other parts of speech. Adjectives and adverbs usually impart the most prejudice or influence to a story — they imply or contain a judgement.

Sometimes adjectives and adverbs signal your approval or disapproval of the subject to the reader. They can also provide 'colour' to a feature story if that is what you desire. But these modifiers should be avoided if you aim to be neutral in a news story. Note the flavour the adjectives and adverbs impart to the examples below, and how different each story sounds when you remove them:

**Fifty-two <u>angry</u> protesters were injured in a <u>serious</u> clash with <u>baton-wielding</u> police outside Parliament yesterday.**

**The Prime Minister <u>brusquely</u> refused to answer <u>numerous</u> <u>searching</u> questions from reporters about the resignation yesterday of the foreign minister.**

**Morals campaigner Verna Doogoode is mounting a <u>nagging</u> campaign to press her <u>insistent</u> demands for a government ban on massage parlours.**

Good editors train themselves to write with nouns and verbs. They only use adjectives and adverbs when appropriate — to define, clarify or provide colour. Otherwise avoid them and employ powerful verbs to carry the story. Think of the verb as the **engine** of the sentence — the better the engine is tuned, the better the car's performance. And remember that the *Lord's Prayer*, one of the most powerful pieces of prose ever written, contains only one adjective.

In news subbing, adjectives and adverbs fall into two categories that I call relevant and irrelevant. If modifiers contribute information to a story, they are relevant. If they are padding, they need to be removed. Consider this example. You are subbing a story about a car accident in which three people died. In this story, *three* is a relevant adjective. It contributes to the story because it conveys information. But to say that bald people died in the accident contributes little. Similarly, to say that the accident happened 'suddenly' or 'violently' is also irrelevant. Almost all car accidents happen suddenly and involve violence. Irrelevant modifiers only contribute verbiage.

# Advice from Mark Twain

The great American writer Mark Twain said: 'When you catch an adjective, kill it.' He meant that good writers work with nouns, pronouns and verbs, and if you choose the appropriate words you often do not need adjectives. No adjective has been conceived that can rescue an inappropriate noun; no adverb can save a bad verb. Beware prose larded with adjectives and adverbs. Are they relevant? Do they contribute to the story? If not, remove them.

The verbs and nouns in these word pairs on the next page are strong enough to stand on their own. Removing the (underlined) adjectives improves clarity. These are examples of tautologies, a form of unnecessary repetition that good subs would never accept.

<u>brilliant</u> genius

<u>terrible</u> tragedy

<u>proposed</u> plans

<u>honest</u> truth

<u>lifeless</u> corpse

<u>early</u> pioneer

> **Subbing tip: The adjective is the enemy of the noun and the adverb is the enemy of the verb.**

## More advice for journalists

My first chief sub-editor, the late great Denis Butler, had a similar motto to Twain's. In 1976 Butler was the first recipient of the Australian journalist of the year award named in honour of *Age* editor Graham Perkin. One of Butler's favourite phrases was: 'The adjective is the enemy of the noun and the adverb is the enemy of the verb'. He reasoned that journalists need to stick to facts when writing news stories. Keep Twain's and Butler's advice close to your heart. You will be a better editor.

### A tip about weak verbs

The verbs 'to be', 'to make', 'to go' and 'to have' are wonderful words, but in journalistic terms they should be avoided. Bad writers use them in combination with other words to produce weak sentences. Thus we read about thieves who 'made their escape' instead of 'escaped'. Or we hear about people 'taking their leave' when they should have 'left'. A powerful verb can often be found in the obscure phrase, as in the example above where the stronger verb 'escaped' was hiding in the clause 'made their escape'.

Forms of the verb 'to be' appear in the passive voice, so watch out for compound verbs containing 'was' and 'were'. The preposition 'by' often indicates passive phrasing, so be on your guard when you see that word. For example, 'The mat was sat on by the cat' is passive and 'by' gives it away. Never start a sentence with weak words like 'There is' or 'There are' or 'There have been' or 'There were'. These are signs of amateur writing. Beware compound forms of all the weak verbs above and, where appropriate, improve them. For example, a poor writer might say 'The man went home quickly' while a better writer would say 'The man ran home'.

## Trust your inner ear

Subs need to ensure copy is as clear as possible. If you know a sentence is correct but it sounds wrong to your inner ear, then you are probably best to rework the sentence until it is both correct and sounds right. One attribute of a good sub is a love of reading. With time we pick up the rhythms and cadences of good writing, and we know if something sounds right. Learn to trust your inner ear and follow up with a reference book.

# The essence of editing

In Elizabethan times (about 400 years ago) the average prose sentence contained 45 to 50 words. A century ago, the average length was 30 to 35. In modern newspapers sentences average somewhere between 12 and 25 words. We live in an age that wants information quickly. People should not have to re-read sentences to comprehend them. They expect to be able to understand a sentence at first reading. This leads to the essence of editing: You influence your reader's ability to understand what you edit through the length of sentences and the number of syllables in the words of those sentence. Aim for an average sentence length of 15 to 25 words, and aim to use as many words of one or two syllables as possible. Writer George Orwell offered these guidelines in 1946. They are still relevant:

**1.** Never use a metaphor, simile, or other figure of speech that you are used to seeing in print.
**2.** Never use a long word where a short one will do.
**3.** If it is possible to cut a word out, always cut it out.
**4.** Never use the passive where you can use the active.

**5.** Never use a foreign phrase, a scientific word, or a jargon word if you can think of an everyday English equivalent.

**6.** Break any of these rules rather than saying anything outright barbarous.

## One idea per sentence

As a general rule, a sentence should contain one idea. A short sentence is a great aid to clarity. But too many short sentences can sound simplistic if you are not careful. To avoid monotony and to give variety and rhythm, vary the length of your sentences.

# Sentence types

Essentially, there are three basic sentence types. Each has its advantages and disadvantages. Subs should concentrate on using these basic Lego blocks, plus three other (rarer) sentence types discussed later. The three most common sentence types are:

■ Simple

■ Compound

■ Complex

## Simple

The simple sentence has one subject and one object (also known as the predicate) joined by a verb. For example: 'The man (subject) chewed (verb) the chocolate (predicate/object).' Simple sentences convey a mood of action. They give a sense of power. A succession of simple sentences can be powerful. Like the thump of a fist hitting the table. This paragraph consists of simple sentences. Modern newspapers use them often. But too many simple sentences can make prose sound simplistic.

## Compound

A compound sentence consists of two simple sentences linked by a conjunction. The most common conjunctions are 'yet', 'but', 'or', 'and'. Compound sentences are fine if you want to generate a feeling of evenness and suggest a mood of regularity. They are like the rhythm of regular sine curves but they can also be very boring if you use too many. This paragraph contains three successive compound sentences to generate a sense of rhythm, but too many can make you seasick.

## Complex

The complex sentence has one main statement, usually a simple sentence, and one or more subordinate statements, also known as clauses, which contribute to the main statement. The previous sentence is an example. The main statement is 'The complex sentence has one main statement' and the three subordinate clauses make up the rest of the sentence. How do you distinguish between a sentence and a clause? A sentence contains a verb and makes sense on its own, which is why it is also called an independent clause. A clause similarly contains a verb but it does not make sense on its own. A collection of words that contains a verb but cannot stand on its own is called a dependent clause.

You will also find a rare and sophisticated complex sentence known as a compound-complex sentence. Use these sparingly, as seldom as possible, because they are usually complicated and can become confusing — often too confusing for most readers — and they tend to ramble, as this example of a compound-complex sentence is beginning to ramble, which almost inevitably causes comprehension problems for your reader.

Good construction consists mostly of using simple and compound sentences, with the occasional sprinkling of spice in the form of a complex sentence. Three other types of sentence, discussed below, provide another form of condiment. As with any spice, use sparingly. The three other sentence types are:

- Periodic
- Balanced
- Loose

## Periodic

Periodic sentences build to a climax. The main impact is held back until the end. They are attractive to readers if used occasionally because periodic sentences keep the suspense to the last moment. Here is an example, with acknowledgement to the original advertisement in which it appeared.

**Even at 100 miles an hour, the only sound that can be heard behind the wheel of the latest Rolls Royce is the tick of the electric clock.**

## Balanced

These are works of deliberate symmetry. You have to work hard to create them. They have a literary feel, as in this description of the boxer Joe Louis that reporter Bob Considine coined during the bout between Louis and Max Schmeling in New York in 1938:

**He was a big, lean copper spring, tightened and re-tightened through weeks of training until he was one pregnant package of coiled venom.**

## Loose

These run on from fact to fact in almost a conversational sequence, a bit like water over a waterfall. Sometimes they work, but be careful because they can seem sloppy. They roll on and on and often do not reach a climax. Sometimes you need to be savage and insert a full point to control them. One useful subbing tip here is to locate any conjunctions, delete them and insert a full stop. This description of an election-night party contains an example of a loose sentence:

**People on the phones were gabbling in a variety of languages, cameras and camera crews milling around the main entrance, and snappily-dressed minders around the politicians, with harassed members of the general press corps squirming in their seats in the reception area waiting to interview the winners.**

You could easily improve this sentence by inserting a few full stops:

People gabbled in a variety of languages on the phones. Camera crews milled around the main entrance. Snappily-dressed minders kept guard around the politicians. Reporters squirmed in their seats in the reception area waiting to interview the winners.

# The basic principles of editing

Editing involves basic principles. One way to remember them is to have an image of a passkey. Think of it as the passkey to success as a sub and as a guide to the principles of good prose writing. When editing, make sure you make the copy you handle:

- Positive
- Active
- Specific
- Simple
- Concise

> You influence a reader's ability to understand what you edit through the *length* of sentences and the *number of syllables* in the words of those sentences.

## Positive

One job of a news story is to tell readers what has happened. People are generally not interested in what has not happened. The only exceptions are those rare occasions when you need to highlight the negative, such as when a country votes no in a referendum or a council rejects a proposal. Sentences should assert. Subs need to learn to express negatives in a positive way. Thus instead of writing:

**Mikael Paznewski, who escaped from Barwon prison last week, has still not been apprehended.**

you should say

**Mikael Paznewski is still on the run after escaping from Barwon prison last week.**

And instead of:

**The company says it will not now proceed with the new management plan.**

you could say

**The company has abandoned the management plan.**

# Active

Orwell maintains that writing should be in the active voice as much as possible. As you know, this is where the subject performs the action, rather than having the action done to it. The latter is known as the passive voice. Why should journalists avoid passive construction? Because active voice is clearer, more concise and tends to mimic the natural human style of conversation. As the name suggests, it is more 'active'.

Here is an example of passive phrasing:

**It was deemed appropriate that a meeting of the businessmen would be held next week.**

Passive voice is a cunning way to say little in a lot of words. It also leaves questions unanswered in the reader's mind. In the example above, who considered it appropriate to hold the meeting? A good sub would pen something like:

**The businessmen agreed to meet next week.**

## A warning

When editing copy to ensure it is positive and in the active voice, you will need to take care to clarify points of information. Passive voice and negative phrasing are a haven for muddled thinking and confusion. Reporters who do not know the facts fudge stories. A sub must understand the story she or he is subbing. You will need to ask questions of reporters, and you will need to be persistent to get full details. Encourage reporters to include phone numbers with their copy in case you need to ask questions.

Take the example on this and the previous page of the company that decided it would not proceed with the management plan. Before you could write that it had *abandoned* its plan you would need to know if the company had actually abandoned the project. Perhaps it had delayed for a month (in which case you would need to write that it had *postponed* its plans).

Or perhaps it was holding fire on the project and would reintroduce it when the economic climate improved (in which case you would write that it had *shelved its plans until the economic climate improved*). Subs need to have a feeling for language and to know what words mean.

## Specific

Specific writing involves using common nouns and powerful verbs, and avoiding vague terms such as abstract nouns. People relate to things through their senses — they like to read about events they can touch or hear or see. Abstract words tell them nothing and feel unsatisfying. If you write about a mode of production used for the transportation of weathered igneous material, you will confuse readers. Better to talk about a shovel. And why write:

**The theatre has seating accommodation for 600 people.**

When you could just as easily say:

**The theatre seats 600.**

## Simplicity

Clear writing is simple writing. The best writers in English have known that elegance is contained in simplicity. It is also the best way to be understood. A full stop is one of the best ways to simplify a sentence. One idea per sentence is the ideal for clear writing. Sentences should travel without excess baggage. If you choose the right nouns and verbs, you seldom need adverbs and adjectives. If you use modifiers, make sure they contribute to the story.

Rudolph Flesch suggests that comprehension levels fall when writers use too many words of more than three syllables. That is why editors should use simple words, and explains Orwell's advice to prefer the short word to the long. Instead of the bloated words in the left column below you should employ those on the right.

altercation    fight

apprehend    catch

| abrasions | cuts |
| --- | --- |
| conflagration | fire |
| terminate | end |

Similarly, what does this gobbledygook mean?

**A domestic accommodation amelioration programme has been instigated by the National Australia Bank in an attempt to improve the standard of housing in Yourtown. Grants of up to $20,000 will be made available to suitably-qualified people.**

Surely the reporter means:

**The National Australia Bank is offering loans of up to $20,000 for home improvement in Yourtown.**

## Concise

A secret to writing well is choosing the best combination of words. The French phrase *le mot juste* summarizes this idea — the right words in the right order. Concise writing avoids verbal clutter. You do this in two ways. The first is selection of specific and concrete terms. The second is to know the value of words, so that each word carries its own weight.

Thus instead of the horrors on the left, you should prefer those on the right:

| posed a question | asked |
| --- | --- |
| made a contribution | gave |
| gained an insight | realized |
| tendered her resignation | quit |

# Lessons from the *Bible*

We can learn a lot from reading simple English. Subs could do worse than read some of the great books, including the *Bible*, to get a feel for great writing. And like a literary form of osmosis, with time you might find the rhythms and cadence of fine writing seeping into your literary pores. The first book of the *Bible*, Genesis, does not begin with: 'An amazingly exciting account of how one solitary individual, single-handed and unaided, brilliantly created the entirety of the world in the incredibly short period of six 24-hour peregrinations.' No, Genesis simply says: 'In the beginning, God created the heavens and the Earth.' It is fine journalism because it is positive, active, simple, specific and concise: In the beginning (when) God (subject) created (verb) the heavens and the Earth (object). The time element starts the sentence because it is significant to the story.

# Exercises

**1. Rewrite these sentences to remove the negative expression.**

The politician did not pay attention to the electorate's concerns.

It has not stopped raining for the past six days.

The refugees were not allowed any food during their 20-day ordeal.

Many critics regarded Bloggs as not generous with his employees.

All six members of the records department were not retained after a review by their employer, Sir Horace Hobknob.

**2. Rewrite these sentences in the active voice.**

New sales objectives were posted by the company's CEO, Sir Cyril Snapp.

The clothing prices were reduced 50 per cent by Myer at the sale.

The Stock Exchange's report confirmed what had long been suspected by the fraud squad — widespread bribery among brokers.

There have been reports by the FBI that religious cults have been formed by journalism academics across Victoria.

Fire insurance policies are offered to large corporations by all insurance companies.

**3. Edit these sentences to make them clearer and simpler.**

He suffered the loss of his right eye.

Not until late August did she finally receive the money.

The blaze initiated at about midnight in the vicinity of the Geelong High School.

A hospital spokesman said it was hoped that the medical programme would be entirely self-supporting.

Car sales are decreasing because of the fact that the vehicles are becoming more expensive, the economist said.

**4. Improve these sentences by finding stronger verbs.**

The club was on the lookout for more members.

The consensus of opinion among participants in the workshop was that formal classes in sex education were a necessity for high school students.

Another practice the radio station allegedly engaged in was to bill customers twice for the same advertisements.

Speaking of the plan, the minister said what it would do would be to give the elderly more protection against the problem of inflation.

Financial problems were listed as one of the reasons why the city has decided to abandon its plans to expand the school.

**5. These sentences have awkward passive phrasing. Rewrite them in the active voice.**

The book on management was read by our top executives.

The performance appraisals were scheduled for the first three months of the year by our boss.

There have been reports by the FBI and CIA that religious cults have been formed by journalism academics across Australia.

My new schedule was arranged yesterday by my secretary.

Attention was taken from the positive aspects of the proposal by the minister's press secretary.

6. Identify the sole adjective in the *Lord's Prayer*.

# References

Orwell, George (1961). 'Politics of the English language' in *Collected Essays*. London: Secker & Warburg.

Paterson, Mike in Tucker, Jim (1992). *Kiwi Journalist: A practical guide to news journalism*. Auckland: Longman.

Shertzer, Margaret (1986). *The Elements of Grammar*. New York: Macmillan.

Strunk, William and White, E.B. (1979). *The Elements of Style*. Third edition. New York: Macmillan.

Venolia, Jan (1987). *Rewrite Right: How to revise your way to better writing*. San Francisco: Ten Speed Press.

# How to write compelling headlines

## Summary

■ Headline constraints: Time and space

■ How to write effective headlines

■ Avoiding labels

■ Dangers of ambiguity and puns

■ Ways to refine headlines

■ Headline size and shape

■ A suggested procedure for writing headlines

**M**OST newspaper readers look first at large images — usually photographs and their captions and other large graphics — and then the headlines. Why? Because they are the most striking visual elements on a page. When readers select what stories to read, their decision is usually based on the impact of the headline and the graphics. The visual elements of editing are discussed in Chapters 6 and 7. This chapter concerns itself with writing headlines that make people want to read the accompanying stories. The next chapter looks at writing powerful captions because this is a key skill required of all subs. Generally new subs cut their teeth on copy editing before they get to design pages. That is why we begin with headlines and captions (known as cutlines in the United States). With headlines we will start with two key questions:

**1.** What is the headline's role?

**2.** What makes a good headline?

We have already started looking at the answer to the first question. Eyetrack research shows that readers' eyes go first to photos and display type — the large headlines. If the display type captures their interest, they may move on to the body type. The managing editor of *The Sunday Oregonian*, Jack Hart, suggests that the odds are about 5-1 against a reader finishing the story they start. 'We're fighting a resistant audience under the best of circumstances. So the importance of the display type cannot be emphasized enough. Copyediting gurus repeatedly proclaim it is the most important writing in the paper. If our most important objective is just to get folks to read the paper, they're absolutely right.'

Hart is pointing out that readers are time poor. Most newspaper readers are browsers because few have the time or inclination to read every word in a publication. They select what appeals or what they consider relevant. One of the headline's roles, then, is to tell readers about the story's content, or to tease them if the headline refers to an offbeat or funny story. In the former case, the *Financial Times*, which publishes in London, Frankfurt, Hong Kong and the United States, expects the headline and the first three paragraphs to tell the gist of the story. The paper caters for the needs of its readers, who are perceived to be busy people. The situation changes on weekends, or when people think they have more leisure time. But on daily papers or Web sites, most readers are browsers. This should influence how we build headlines.

Headlines have several other purposes. As Hart notes, they are necessary as a major visual attraction. They also break up slabs of grey body text. They usually fit into a particular shape to follow the publication's design philosophy, and they are an effective way of organizing a group of related stories. The publication's tone and the perceived audience will also influence the type of headline. A headline that works for a Sunday tabloid story will look ridiculous over a similar story in a serious broadsheet, even though both may be well crafted. The role of a good headline, then, is to:

■ draw or grab the reader into the body of the story

■ tell the reader what the story is about

■ provide information in a digestible and/or entertaining form.

In some respects, the answers to the two questions we began with are the same, though you could argue any response to the second question is more open to debate. While we cannot follow a formula for writing a good headline, we can apply basic principles. The first part of this chapter develops these principles. The rest of the chapter looks at ways to refine your headlines, and it concludes with a process for writing them. We will begin with the principles, but first we need to consider the two primary constraints on headlines — time and space.

# Headline constraints:
# Time and space

News subs are generally always working against the clock to produce 'live' pages — those being prepared for the next edition. On all 49 Australian dailies, news subs are working in the evening to prepare the paper for the next edition, which is the next morning. On most New Zealand dailies it is that afternoon — 18 of the 25 Kiwi dailies are afternoon editions. In the United States as of early 1999, 721 dailies were morning publications and 781 published in the evening. In the UK, all but one of the London-based nationals appear in the morning, while many of the regional dailies are afternoon publications.

The other constraint is space. News headlines are almost always written to fit an allocated space. I say almost because some tabloid front pages are designed around a pre-written head. Most headlines are governed by width and depth. Whatever the typeface, the sub-editor is restricted to a certain number of characters and a certain number of lines (known as decks). Obviously the larger the type, the fewer the characters that can be accommodated. (As an exercise, take a look at the kinds of type books used in 'hot metal' — old technology days — to see how subs used to have to calculate character counts over various column widths by hand.) Nowadays, page designers place these details electronically in the format for each story. You might see, for example, that you have to write a headline three columns wide over two lines or decks using a specific typeface. The typeface and column width will influence the number of characters in a headline. Using the example above, a three-column headline in 36pt Helvetica bold means you have a maximum of 21.5 characters for each deck — that's about four words per line over the 36 ems of the three columns. Chapter 5 covers typography and ems.

Lack of space makes headline writing a real skill; indeed, many would argue that it is an art. Harold Evans maintains that headline writing is the sub's major skill. Now let us look at some principles involved in creating headlines.

# How to write effective headlines

As a general guide, headlines need to be written:

- in present tense
- in active voice
- with a personal tone

Because of space constraints, every word must earn its place. You can do that by keeping your headlines:

- simple
- precise
- positive

Other ways to improve headlines include remembering to:

- employ powerful verbs
- concentrate on one main point
- use key words

## Principle 1: Present tense

Most headlines are written in the present tense because it gives a sense of immediacy. It is the same reason that broadcast news is almost always written in the present tense. It brings the action to the reader and involves them in the drama. Because of the way English is constructed, present tense also tends to be shorter.

Consider this scenario: Two jets get in each other's way while preparing for take-off and 50 people are injured. A novice might construct this headline:

## 50 were injured
## when jets
## were in collision

We replace the past with the present tense, and also prefer words that convey a sense of immediacy ('as' instead of 'when'). We also use the verb 'collide' instead of the phrase 'in collision'. So the headline reads:

## 50 are injured
## as jets
## collide

In practice, the verb to be should almost always be implied (the rare exception should occur only when we need to pad a head to fill the given space). We get:

## 50 hurt
## as jets
## collide

This is an accurate headline and appropriate for a broadsheet, but a tabloid paper might consider it dreary. The collision took place early today and tonight's TV news will probably do the story to death. Our story will not appear until tomorrow, so we need to enliven the action. We have made it sound immediate by taking the reader to the scene. Now we aim to give it some oomph. The type of oomph will depend on the perceived tone of your publication. A racy tabloid might write:

## Panic on runway, 50 hurt

## Principle 2: Active voice

Use the active voice as often as possible. The same principle applies when editing body copy. Active voice, where the subject performs the action rather than having the action done to it, has two major advantages — it uses fewer words than passive voice and it makes the headline more immediate, which implies urgency. It is also more natural because it sounds more conversational.

Consider this scenario: Masked men enter a suburban bank, blow away the manager with a shotgun when he tries to stop them and steal $200,000. You could write:

## Bank manager gunned down by masked men

This headline is mediocre. The passive voice slows it down and makes it sound stuffy. Worst of all, it takes too long to find out who did the shooting. The active voice is more vital and also allows room for more information. Better to write:

## Gunmen blast bank manager, take $200,000

Occasionally you can extract more impact by using passive phrasing. The trick is to drop the auxiliary parts of the verb and imply the action — here you are really saying the banker *was shot* dead. You could pen:

**Banker dead
as gunmen
grab $120,000**

Consider another scenario: The All Blacks manage a big win over the Wallabies in a third and deciding rugby test. A novice sub might try to be cute and compose this appalling appellation of atrocious assonance and alliteration (oops):

**Wallabies
walloped
by All Blacks**

Better to avoid the cute alliteration and passive phrasing and write:

**All Blacks          All Blacks
take test           thrash
and series          Wallabies**

## Principle 3: Aim to personalize

Newspaper readers are interested in what happens to people. People make news. Abstracts put readers to sleep.

Here is a scenario: Marauding youths terrorize a grocer in Toorak, one of Melbourne's more salubrious suburbs. An inexperienced sub might write:

**Youths attack
Toorak store**

This headline is bland and silly because it suggests the schoolboys attacked an inanimate object. The headline also lacks any local feel. If you can use a person or place name to represent a general principle, it is generally better to do so. This principle especially applies for community newspapers and regional dailies because readers identify with their neighbourhood or community. An alert sub on the Toorak community paper would write:

**Youths savage**     or     **Toorak terrors**
**Toorak grocer**            **attack grocer**

## Principle 4: Use precise language

Inexperienced or sloppy subs are often happy if the head fits, even though the words are imprecise. Indeed, there may be times for all of us when we are happy with any reasonable head because the revise sub is screaming for the page. But you must spurn vague or imprecise words.

Good subs craft headlines in unambiguous language, using common and proper nouns and avoiding abstract nouns. Let us say the federal government cuts tax on new cars and trucks. This triple-decker is too vague, and its shape is ugly (shapes are discussed later in the chapter).

**Major cuts in taxes**
**on new vehicles**

What does 'major' mean for your readers? What are 'vehicles'? If the 20 per cent tax cut represents $5,000 for each new car, then say so:

**$5,000 tax cut**
**on new cars**

Similarly, if burglars steal a prominent actor's jewels (and they are valued at $2 million), it would be easy and tempting to write:

## VIP's valuable
## jewels stolen

But what does 'valuable' mean? The word is too vague — it means different things to different readers, depending on their income. Who is the VIP? Be precise and personalize. If the actor is well known, say Nicole Kidman, a better headline would say:

## Kidman laments
## $2m gems loss

Often if we want to personalize, it is difficult avoiding the passive but we can get around the problem by implying the passive. We leave it to the reader to infer that it must have been thieves who did the stealing. Thus:

## Kidman's $2m
## jewels stolen

Never try to boost a story by adding words like *valuable* or *great* or *well-known* or *important*. These adjectives are relative. What is important to one person may be unimportant to another. Be precise. Give the figure or the fact or the detail or the size. Leave it to the reader to decide the importance or value of an event. For the same reason, you should never introduce terms like *horror* or *tragedy* in stories about death or destruction.

# Avoiding labels

One of the easiest ways to write a headline in a hurry is to slap on a label. It may work if you are desperate and on a deadline. But labels are seldom precise. They produce boring headlines. They also sound predictable. Here is a scenario: It is the Liberal party's annual conference. It happens every year

and not much seems to be happening in the story you are subbing. You are tempted to stick on a label. It could easily end up
a yawn like:

## Liberals' yearly get together

The solution is to dig out something of interest from the
report and give the headline a strong verb. If, in the scenario
above, the conference calls for conscription to be resumed to
reduce unemployment, you could pen these glorious words:

## Conscription works, Liberal meeting told

## Principle 5: Tell a simple story

One of the headline's jobs is to provide the essence of the story.
Some subs try to cram in too much detail and tell too much.
This produces the aberration of the noun–adjective headline,
where nouns masquerading as adjectives produce a string of
statements, usually without a verb. These constipated collec-
tions of words confuse readers. You have probably read these
types of heads in papers where the sub had limited space.

## Divorce deal survey shock

or

## Wives swap charge in night shift case

You do not need to tell *all* the story in the heading. Select
the essence of the action and use that as the basis for your
head. Stick to one message and do it well. Information overload is cruelty to readers. Write headlines with nouns and
verbs. Avoid irrelevant adjectives. It helps if you keep the words
simple and natural by using everyday terms. Avoid confusing

words or terms that do not occur in ordinary dialogue. Most people would puzzle over this example:

**New non-recyclable products eschewed**

# Dangers of ambiguity and puns

Generally it is best to avoid deliberate ambiguity, such as puns, unless the story cries out for it — an odd spot, for example. As ever, your publication's tone and style should help you decide. The subs who wrote the examples below probably thought they were funny, but readers probably thought otherwise.

**'Staggering' attendance at church**

**Three battered in fish shop**

**Sewer row: Minister steps in**

## Principle 6: Use powerful verbs

If your headline sounds bland, you are probably using bland verbs. The verb is the engine of a headline. An excellent way to boost a headline is to introduce a more powerful verb. Let us say you receive this story: Four people died when a car crashed and caught fire at the intersection of Main highway and High Road in Yourtown, bringing the national road toll to 101. It would be acceptable to write:

**Four die in Yourtown car crash**

But the headline could be so much better. Look for a stronger verb and add a dash of flair, and you get:

**Road deaths** or **Crash kills**
**nudge 100** **4 as toll**
**as 4 perish** **tops ton**

Vivid verbs create word pictures for the reader. Supply some exciting images for the picture shows in readers' heads. The headline below is too nebulous and commits many of the sins condemned earlier in the chapter:

**Big storms cause**
**chaos in city**

Get some action and detail on to the page. Employ a muscular verb and include some facts:

**$3m of damages**
**as gales lash city**

You can make any story more interesting by taking an unusual angle and looking for a powerful verb. But keep the headline simple. Readers should never have to reread a headline to understand it. And ensure the facts support your stronger wording. Make sure it was a gale and not just a storm.

# Ways to refine headlines

So far we have looked at the basic principles for writing headlines. Now we move on to some refinements — ways to improve your heads, plus some more things to avoid. The definite and indefinite articles — *the, an* and *a* — can generally be implied, just as you imply the tense of some verbs (see principle one).

Dropping articles saves words and usually makes it possible to read the headline more quickly. (The only time you might include the definite or indefinite article is to pad a headline to fit the required space.) You should never employ a head like:

## The mayor's house
## is hit by a storm

This is a slight improvement:

## Mayor's house
## hit by storm

But it is far better to use an active version:

## Storm destroys
## mayor's house

Note: When pruning a head, be sure to retain the indefinite or definite article where its omission could lead to confusion.

## Paterson says
## journalism is
## way to the top

In the headline above, is Mike Paterson suggesting that journalism is the *only* way to the top, or merely one way? If it is the former, we need to include the definite article 'the'; if it is the former we could include the indefinite article 'a'. Best to use the definite or indefinite article, or another word to remove confusion, as in the examples below.

| | | |
|---|---|---|
| **Paterson says** **journalism is** **a way to the top** | versus | **Paterson says** **journalism is** **best way to top** |

Note: Avoid using the indefinite or definite articles even to fill space. It looks cluttered and the headline reads like someone talking with a mouthful of cracker biscuits. Better to rewrite the head. Let us look at other things to avoid. Take care with:

■ Compound verbs

■ Abbreviations

■ Excess punctuation

■ Capitals

■ Clichés

## Compound verbs

People read headlines one deck at a time, so ensure that each makes sense on its own. Phrase headlines line by line and listen to them with your inner ear. Be especially careful when using compound verbs or nouns in a multi-deck headline. In particular, beware ending the top line with a word that can be a noun or a verb. Disasters occur when the compound noun or verb trips over into the next line. Here is a classic that appeared during World War II (though I suspect it may have been intentional).

## Allied troops'
## push bottles
## up Kraut rear

## Abbreviations and initials

Lack of space sometimes forces subs to use ugly abbreviations. Only a handful are easy to read or are sufficiently well known to be instantly recognized. Even a common abbreviation like TV can be written three ways. Abbreviations confuse the reader and they also look ugly on a page. Is ltd as easy to read or as attractive as company or group? Is govt as easy to absorb as Blair or Howard or Gore or Bush?

As a general rule, use as few abbreviations as possible. If you find yourself putting abbreviations in a headline, rewrite the headline. Apply the same rule with initials and acronyms.

They mean different things to different groups. To a camera buff, SLR refers to a type of camera. To a soldier, SLR is a type of rifle. To a student of African politics, SLR was an African independence movement.

Always consider the knowledge limits of your reader. This headline confused even the good citizens of Melbourne:

## WEF to meet next week in Melbourne

## Punctuation

Be careful with commas. The simple omission of one comma changes the meaning of these headlines, and may make the second version defamatory.

| | | |
|---|---|---|
| **Pathetic, mayor condemns rates increase** | versus | **Pathetic mayor condemns rates increase** |

Avoid using a comma in place of *and* unless you absolutely must. Better to rewrite the headline. In this example:

### Dice loaded against independents, minority parties

the comma was meant to replace 'and'. But it could be read to mean that the minority parties are making the statement, with the comma indicating the start of the attribution.

Exclamation marks should never be used. In the trade they are known as shrieks or dog's dicks. Often they are a proud sub's way of showing he has written a funny headline, and wants to announce it to the world. Too often it is a case of a sub writing a headline to impress other subs. A witty headline does not need crutches.

Strictly speaking, question marks should appear only at the end of a question. But they are useful ways of indicating uncertainty or speculation. For example:

## Rain for final test?

is acceptable if it alerts the reader of possible rain for the test match. Similarly,

## Election in March?

tells readers that a national election is likely in March. If the report makes this clear, you are probably right to use a question mark in this case.

Another punctuation mark — the dash — can be useful to indicate attribution. But it can look ugly on tight column measures and it can be abrupt and awkward for readers who are not used to it. This headline appeared in the *New Zealand Herald* over two columns (18 ems) at the size shown.

# Distortion — Bolger

It is an excellent example of how *not* to use a dash because the headline says almost nothing. Bolger was prime minister in the early 1990s.

If you include a quote in a headline, most style books tell you to use single quotes because they save space. Double quote marks look ugly and take up too much space. Quote marks can also be used to indicate doubt about the truth of a word or to reverse the meaning of the word quoted. For example:

## 'Lost' boy safe in bed

## 'Dead' man at own funeral

## Capitals

Capitals are an excellent way to make a word or phrase stand out. But they present more problems than they are worth. Capitals are difficult to read, take up to 30 per cent more space compared with upper and lower case headlines, and they can confuse. Notice what happens in these all-caps headlines where the full points have been dropped:

**KEEP OUT OF**      **KEEP OUT OF**
**MURUROA,**        **MURUROA,**
**FRANCE**             **FRANCE**
**TELLS U.S.**        **TELLS US**

As a general rule *avoid* capitals for headlines, if only because they are more difficult to read and take up too much space. Be discreet and intelligent in your use of capitalized words in headlines. If you do use them, be very careful with words like WHO, POW, TAB and US. Most style books tend to turn other acronyms such as QANTAS and NATO into words — Qantas and Nato. Take care not to use all capital headlines which involve place names. Otherwise you get:

**DEAD MAN**      **TWO DIE**
**TURNS UP**       **IN BATH**
**IN ORANGE**

## A word on clichés

Poor writing is easy to recognize because it is usually full of tired expressions and clichés. Headlines that contain clichés are even worse because they are so obvious. Please never let me hear tales of:

## Heart break mums

or read about a:

## Council's green light for plan

# Headline size and shape

Other factors apart from the words need to be considered when writing headlines. As a general rule, the size of a heading reduces as stories move down the page. This design method is used to indicate the decreasing importance of the stories. See Chapter 5 for a discussion on headline typography.

Over the years, subs and designers have experimented with headline shapes. These have included the stepped and inverted pyramid shapes. *The New York Times* still uses them, though they look archaic. With the stepped head, the objective is to have each deck the same length, with each deck indented an increasing distance to give a stepped appearance. The main problem with this style is the need to write lines that are the same length, which consumes valuable time.

**Zzzzz zzzz**
   **zzz zzzzz**
     **zzzz zzzz**

With the inverted pyramid shape, the aim here is to decrease the number of characters in each deck by an even amount, to create the shape of an inverted pyramid. Again, this uses valuable time.

**Zzzzzzzzzz**
   **zzzzzzz**
   **zzzzz**

## Flush left

By far the best approach to composing sensible headlines is to make them flush left with an indent of an en or em (about a quarter to a half centimetre; details in Chapter 5). The indent provides a little extra white space around the headline and makes it easier to read. Thus:

**Zzzzz zzzz**
**zzzz zz**
**zzzzz zzz**
**zzzz zzz**

Flush left provides the most characters for writing the headline, and it uses the eye's natural tendency when reading to return to the left margin to start each new line. It also takes less time than the earlier styles. This is why I believe that flush left is the best standard form for headline shapes. Almost all heads in this book are set left.

In a multi-deck headline, the first line should be longer or the longest. Remember that readers approach headlines one deck at a time. So make sure that each deck makes sense on its own. Some designers like four-deck headlines to appear long, short, long, short as shown above.

## Character count

Before computerized typesetting, subs needed to know how to count characters. They learned that headlines containing 'm' and 'w' occupy more space than headlines using standard-sized letters. Similarly, headlines that contain thin letters such as 'i', 'j', 'l' and 't' permit more characters over a fixed space. These principles still apply with computerized typesetting. Knowing them will help when you need to choose words in cases where you must lose a character to make a headline fit.

In the examples below, two different (fictitious) headlines occupy the same space — yet one contains seven more characters than the other.

## Ways and means

(12 characters plus two spaces)

## Little's title trials

(19 characters plus two spaces)

# A suggested procedure for writing headlines

This section is not intended as a formula for writing headlines. But it is a suggested process for novices. Writing headlines is creative, and various teachers of creativity believe that creativity should start with learning a process. The great acting teacher Stanislavsky maintained that creativity begins with imitation. That is, you should model successful processes until you have mastered the process in your own way. That is the approach taken here.

The first thing to do is to read the story you're subbing until you are clear what it is about. If necessary, read the story several times. But make sure you understand it. Some subs write the headline first after they have read the story. Novices should not do that. Better to sub the body copy first and then write the headline because the process of subbing body text will help you understand the story better. Your subconscious will be working on possible heads.

## A sample checklist
❑ main headline

❑ supplementary headline/s

❑ caption/s

❑ writer's byline

❑ photographer's byline/s

❑ run-on line/s

❑ other unusual features

## Jot down key words

Choose the main idea of the story. Jot down key words. Often you can copy them from the story. Write a trial headline and get your terminal to fit the head. See how many characters you are over or under. Then it is a process of substituting words and ideas to find the best possible head in the available time. Apply the principles outlined thus far in this chapter.

With practice it becomes easier. Until then, aim to stay relaxed. Tension kills creativity. If your mind seizes up, take a break. Get a glass of water, stretch your limbs, check some details in the story in the library or a reference book — anything to take your conscious mind off the issue. Your subconscious mind, meanwhile, is working on the task. But stay calm. Take lots of deep breaths.

Often you will need to cut the story, or expand it to fit a particular space. Tips on editing body text are included in the previous chapter. You may also need to write captions for photographs and provide bylines for the writer and photographer, plus credits for other pictures not taken by staff people. Sometimes you will need to write run-on lines (the words at the end of the first part of the story that say 'continued page 7').

If you are new to subbing, it is useful to keep a checklist (see the previous page for an example). You can tick off each item as you complete it. Keep a note of each headline you write to compare your original with what appears on the page proofs or in print. If they are the same, it is a good indication that you are on the right track. As they get close to deadline, some chief or check subs are too busy to tell new subs where they're going wrong. So checking what appears may be your best way of correcting yourself. If your heads are continually changed, have a chat with the chief or revise sub at a quiet time. As discreetly as possible, ask why they made the changes.

Book Three of Harold Evans's series *Editing and Design* contains an alphabetic list of subjects with a variety of suggested words that are ideal for headlines. Look up the subject you need to use in your headline (listed alphabetically) and read the suggested list of shorter options. For example, under the subject amalgamate (v) we have the words: combine, bond, fuse, join, link, merge, mix, team up, tie, unify, unite, weld.

# Exercises

1. Spend time on the subs' desk of a newspaper or magazine. This time, write a 300-word report on what you learned.

2. Ask a friend to cut some stories from your local paper, without the headline but with the space and type specifications noted. Write headlines for these stories, then compare what you wrote with what appeared in the paper. What did you learn from the exercise?

3. As you read newspapers, study the headlines. Ask yourself, why did the sub-editor choose that combination or words? Can you improve on the headlines you saw?

4. Do the same for captions you read in newspapers. Can you improve them?

5. Compile a list of 20 powerful action verbs. Spend half an hour finding synonyms for those verbs. Compare your list with the list of another student or colleague who was looking for another list of synonyms.

# References

Evans, Harold (1974). *Editing & Design* (Book Three — *News headlines)*. London: Heinemann.

Gibson, Martin (1979). *Editing in the Electronic Era.* Iowa State University Press.

Goltz, Gene (1987). 'The eyes have it: Another readership research tool is introduced' in *Presstime*, September 1987, 14–17.

Hodgson, F.W. (1993). *Subediting: A handbook of modern newspaper editing and production.* Oxford: Focal Press.

Sellers, Leslie (1972). *The Simple Subs Book.* Oxford: Pergamon Press.

Stanislavsky, Konstantin (1937, reprinted 1986). *An actor prepares.* Harmondsworth: Penguin Books.

 # Captions: Text and pictures combined

## Summary

■ Get all the facts

■ Types of captions

■ The golden rule: Be interesting

■ Identify everyone

■ Tips for better captions

■ Caption writing in a nutshell

ANYONE who can write good captions will be a treasured member of a subs' table. This chapter shows you how to combine text with pictures. But first some rules. Every photograph needs a caption. Never publish a picture without some identification, even if it is just one line showing a person's name. Never assume that readers will recognize a face. Often when they do, they cannot remember the name.

Given that most photographs in publications involve people, you must identify all the people in an image. This may be an incentive for limiting the number of people in a picture — that is, cropping and then expanding the image. More on that in Chapter 7, picture editing.

# Get all the facts

How do we write effective captions? Firstly, make sure you have all the facts. The best image in the world still needs a caption. Even the most creative caption writer needs accurate information with which to perform. A good photographer will always supply background details such as name, age and location. But you cannot always be certain this information is correct.

Two ways to improve your chances are to make sure photographers are properly briefed and to give them a fact sheet. In the first case, have the assigning editor or chief of staff tell the photographer why they want any particular photos and the kinds of ways they might be used. If you are not sure, tell them to get horizontal *and* vertical shots, and to limit the number of people in the pictures. If your publication likes to make money by selling news photographs, then you will need to make arrangements for the photographer to take extra, non-news shots. With digital cameras this should not be a problem because costs for peripherals like film and paper are no longer an issue.

In the second case, insist photographers complete a fact sheet for each assignment. This will probably involve negotiating between the subs' table and the person in charge of photographers but it is a worthwhile investment of effort. Get photographers to attach this form to the back of prints if they still use analogue cameras.

Have the form available electronically if the photographers store digital pictures on a server or hard drive. The form lists all the relevant information for the photograph. If you use paper, have the forms printed in pocket or handbag size (about 8 cm by 8 cm), so photographers can carry them with their equipment. Appendix 2 includes a sample fact sheet.

If a reporter accompanies the photographer, get the reporter to write the caption — after discussing with the chief of staff or news editor the kinds of pictures that are likely to be used. Often the reporter's caption can be used as it is written. If it is not, it serves as an excellent cross-check for the editor against errors in the photographer's details.  If your publication sends photographers out alone — an increasing trend, especially at regional dailies and community newspapers — then the sub will be forced to write the caption based on data the photographer supplied. Given that photographers' talents lie in the area of visual communication, and not necessarily editorial content, this can generate awkward scenarios. Your subs' table will need to establish systems for dealing with this.

# Types of captions

Captions come in three main forms. They can be a simple label for a small picture such as a mug shot (single column head and shoulders); a slightly longer block of text that relates to a larger picture, which is usually associated with a story; or a self-contained story, sometimes known as a picture story or stand-alone caption, where the caption is the story. Let us look at each type.

**1. A label.** This almost always applies to a single-column picture of a person. The picture is usually used to illustrate a story in a minor way, such as a mug shot dropped into a column of text. How much you write will depend on the width of the picture and how many lines you are allowed to work with. In many cases you only have one line. In these situations the caption usually consists of the name, plus a little of what the person has done or said if you have the space.

For example: *Arthur Brown, Lotto winner.*

Or: *Arthur Brown . . . winner of yesterday's $3 million Lotto draw.*

Or: *Arthur Brown: 'I badly needed the money' was his only comment after winning $3 million in yesterday's Lotto draw.*

**2.** A caption that explains the **significance** of the picture. In many publications, perhaps because of the race against the clock, the caption repeats part of the story that accompanies the picture. It often consists of a little of the obvious (what can be seen) plus extra information. This type of caption should (at least briefly) contain all the points the reader needs to know — that is, it must make sense on its own and the reader should not need to read the accompanying story. We are talking about the good old who, what, when, where, why and how. Why? Because many readers look at photos before reading the story. In some cases they move on after looking at the picture and reading the caption.

You may get a burst of inspiration that will bring the picture and the caption to life, or you may have to write it straight. Either way, you need good information. Let us say you are asked to provide a caption for a picture of a girl, aged 10, playing in her first rugby match.

Straight: *Tobi Quinn, 10, makes her rugby debut.*

Bright idea: *Tobi Quinn shows she is a match for boys her own age in a rugby trial for Winchelsea's under 11s at Arthur Daly memorial oval yesterday.*

**3.** A caption that's a **self-contained story**. It should be written like a news story, with the news angle tilted towards the picture. In this type of caption it is often necessary to include words like above or above left to indicate where in the picture you can find the person or thing being read about.

# The golden rule: Be interesting

Captions are some of the most read parts of a newspaper. Studies of how people approach publications show that they look first at major images and display headlines. In the case of pictures, the reader's eye moves through the image to the base, looking for the caption. Because readers gravitate towards captions — often then moving on after looking at pictures and reading captions and headlines — subs should consider caption writing an important part of their job. Aim to make captions as interesting as possible. Even the dullest picture can be made relatively interesting by intelligent cropping and a bright caption. But do not state the obvious. People can see the picture for themselves. Respect their common sense and intelligence and avoid boring them by recounting facts that they can see. Resist the temptation to copy and paste from the body of the story. The best technique, in the jargon of TV journalism, is to write off. That is, do not tell the reader what is in the picture, but give them something else that is beyond the image. Nothing is more boring than: *Joe Bloggs, 70, at the wheel of his new car.*

Why not say: *$250,000 may be a lot for a pensioner to pay for a way to get to church on Sundays, but Joe Bloggs seems happy with his new Ferrari.* Get the picture? Caption writing provides a chance to be creative. Do not squander the opportunity.

Now, not all photographs are prizewinners. How do you brighten up a poor picture? Look at it closely. Search for something that is unique, something that conveys the feel or mood of the scene. Can you find some emotion or feeling in the image? Can you insert useful or interesting information?

## Beware visual clichés

Boring photographs, which are essentially visual clichés, tend to come in one of three forms:

**1.** The image where nothing is happening but you have to make it seem interesting, such as a building.

**2.** The cheque or prize presentation — what some commentators call the 'grip and grin' (see visual clichés in Chapter 7).

**3.** The large group (for example, a board of directors or a gaggle of work colleagues).

Again, in the jargon of TV news writing, write off by adding something beyond what is in the picture. Find something related to the picture. As a general rule, avoid the obvious. Pages 61–62 of Book Four in Evans's *Editing and Design* offers some fine examples of how to compose group shots.

In example 1, an exterior of a building society, you could write: *It may seem quiet but the Yourtown Building Society, whose headquarters are shown above, returned $25 million in pre-tax profit last year. This year the society expects to improve on that figure by 10 per cent.*

In example 2, how do you make the rabble around the prize seem interesting? One suggestion could be: *Another ambulance or a new chemotherapy unit — that is what the prize money from this month's raffle is going to buy for Yourtown hospital. Shown above at the cheque presentation yesterday, from left to right, are . . .*

In example 3 you could write: *The Yourtown Health Fund is the country's third-oldest incorporated health society. Its board of directors has almost 200 years of experience in health care. From left to right are . . .*

# Identify everyone

Make sure you identify all the people in a picture. This is another reason for keeping group shots fairly small — a maximum of, say, four to five. Any more and you need to write a novel to fit in all the names, and the faces are very small when reproduced. If you are naming people from left to right, say so. Pick an obvious starting point and keep your style of naming simple. Avoid phrases like: *Clockwise from 11 o'clock, apart from the chairman who is partly obscured at 3 o'clock , are . . .* Encourage your photographers to take interesting and unusual pictures, but insist they keep them simple for captioning purposes. It is nice to have that board of directors in a circle instead of a boring row, but make sure it is an easily understood circle and not a drunken loop.

Typography is covered in the next chapter. As a general rule for captions, use a different weight to differentiate caption text from body copy, and perhaps even a different font. Bold captions should be used half or one point smaller than Roman type. That is, if your body text is 9pt Times Roman, set your captions in 8.5pt Times bold. If your body text size is

8.5pt Nimrod, you might choose to use 8pt Helvetica bold for the caption. But do not go below 8pt — it is too small to read. Put plenty of white space around the caption by indenting an em both sides (about one cm) if the caption is more than one line. If you have a very wide picture (more than two-thirds of your page width) break your captions into two (or maybe three) columns, especially if the caption runs to more than three or four lines. Otherwise it is just too difficult to read over a wide measure.

Avoid small type for reverse (white type on black background) captions and headlines for pictures — anything under 14pt is too small. If you are combining a story with the picture, put the headline *between* the photo and caption. Small heads get lost if you place them above the picture. This is especially the case if they are in reverse.

# Tips for better captions

Anne Glover of the *St Petersburg Times* in Florida offers some tips for new subs. She suggests that when you join a newspaper, find out how the subs' desk approaches captions. Here are some things to look for, she says: 'Present or past tense? Some newspapers insist on present always. Others take a less rigid approach and let sub-editors decide what suits the photo best. Should the caption repeat all the facts in the story? Your newspaper might have a definite policy of who, what, when, where for all captions. But if not, a good way to view captions is to think of them as being like a link on a Web page — a way to click on that area and find out more information. So if you're looking for more, you don't want to repeat everything that has come before.'

Glover says subs should think of the caption as working in partnership with the headline and other display type. 'If you have described something in the headline already, then pick out some more facts from the story to include in the caption. This works especially well on stories that have multiple pix.'

# Caption writing in a nutshell

Make sure you see the original picture if it is a print. Get a photocopy if you are nearing deadline, in case the original print needs to be taken away to be processed. If your news room uses digital images, make sure you can see the picture in the system. You are a fool to try to write a caption without studying the image closely.

Check and double check all details: names, order of people in the picture, ages, location, date, the event. Take extra care with facts. If defamation occurs because of a picture, it is usually because of the caption.

Check page specifications to see how much space you have for the caption you need to write. Make sure you have enough space to do the job properly. If necessary, negotiate with the page designer for an extra line.

## Captions are like writing intros

Think of writing the caption in the same way you write an introduction, in the sense of getting vital information into it. This should give you a good starting point for your first sentence. As with all introductions, aim to get the important or key words into the opening phrase of the first sentence.

Study the facial expressions. Are they sad? Happy? Jubilant? Quizzical? Devastated? Can you bring any emotions into the picture? Ask yourself: What is the tone or feel of the picture? Aim to capture the atmosphere.

Is there a chance for a play on words? This is acceptable with some captions, though it depends on the tone of the image and related story. Obviously you do not want to use a pun in a photograph of two police officers who have been shot dead.

Remember, in the parlance of writing for TV, to write off. Give the readers something more than what is in the picture. This means you may need to do some research to find that something extra. Captions are a chance to exercise your creativity. Let the Muse soar.

# Exercises

1. Get a friend to cut out some photographs from newspapers without the captions, but provide you with enough detail to write your own version. Use material from publications you admire. Compare what you wrote with what appeared.

2. Practise writing a caption to fit an exact space, such as allowing yourself 160 characters to write a two-line caption for a three-column photograph.

# References

Bowles, Dorothy & Borden, Diane (2000). *Creative Editing*. Third edition. Stamford, CT: Wadsworth. See pages 289–293.

Evans, Harold (1974). *Editing & Design* (Book Four — *Picture on a Page*). London: Heinemann.

Hodgson, F.W. (1993). *Subediting: A handbook of modern newspaper editing and production*. Oxford: Focal Press. See pages 182–185.

Sellers, Leslie (1972). *The Simple Subs Book*. Oxford: Pergamon Press. See pages 118–125.

# 5 Typography: A foundation for design

## Summary

- Typography's influence on legibility
- Measurement of type
- Serif versus sans serif type
- Finding optimum column width
- Styles of typesetting
- Kerning and condensing headlines
- Musings on headline typography

TYPOGRAPHY was once an arcane subject that journalists believed should best be left to printers. But television and computers have changed this situation. Because of television, video and other distractions, we live in a visual age. Readers are much more visually sophisticated. They are unwilling to spend time with a publication they find difficult to read. More recently, computerized production has meant that responsibility for a publication's 'look' has been passed to sub-editors and designers. Typography has always been the foundation stone of publication design. Subs must know something about it because it affects our readers' well-being and, indirectly, those people pay our salaries.

# Typography's influence on legibility

This chapter will look at typography in the context of the changing digital world. Subs need to appreciate how typography — the study and use of typefaces — affects legibility and readability. A publication's choice of typefaces directly influences how easily people read a publication (known as legibility). Type also influences the ease with which people find their way around a publication and how enjoyable they find reading it (known as readability).

Some people may argue that subs do not need to become familiar with typography because computerized production has seen widespread introduction of rigid page templates. Pagination systems can lock in type specifications and the sub may have no control over them. This is simplistic. Subs are in the communication business and this chapter will show that type is a key part of the communication process. Good subs will learn to appreciate the beauty and power of typography, especially if they get the opportunity to design pages from scratch. Let us begin with some definitions and a bit of history.

# Measurement of type

Type is measured in points. Two measurement systems operate around the world: the American, used throughout much of the English-speaking world, and the European. The difference between them is minimal. Australia, Canada, New Zealand and the UK use the American system, though Australia and NZ have adapted it slightly. Typography has its own language. Figure 5.1 on the next page shows the elements that make up a piece of type.

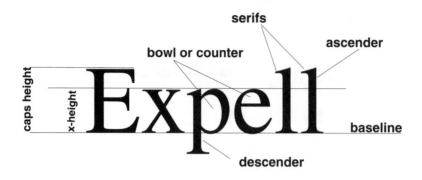

**Figure 5.1: A diagram of a word in 72pt Times Roman, showing the terms that describe a piece of type.**

In hot metal days, when molten lead was poured into moulds to make the (reversed) characters, each piece of type was set on a base of lead, known as a slug. Most publications still use the term 'slug' to label a story — we give it a 'slug line'. In hot metal days this label or name was typed at the top of every take (page) of a story to identify it. If a reporter was writing a story about a robbery, he or she would slug that story 'robbery 1', 'robbery 2' and so on. This enabled several linotype operators to work on various sections of a story when close to deadline.

For simplicity's sake, most people say that there are 72 points to the inch. Actually, 72 points make 0.996264 of an inch. The metric system (centimetres and kilograms) replaced the imperial system (inches and pounds) a generation ago but many people still link points with inches. An inch equals 2.54 centimetres. As you can see from Figure 5.1 above, the metal base was slightly larger than the actual letter. This factor influenced type size.

Point size is measured from the top of the base that contains the letter to the bottom. This means that the printed image of a 72pt capital letter is slightly less than an inch because of the shoulder, the extra distance from the letter to the top of the base. And lower case 72pt letters without an ascender or descender are significantly smaller than capital letters — just over a centimetre. In other words, the point size of a letter has relatively little to do with its actual print size.

## Type in a newspaper context

In the editorial sections of a newspaper, type is used for body text, captions, precedes (story summaries), break-out quotes and headlines (known as display type). Traditionally, body text and captions came in sizes from 5pt through to 10pt in one-point increments, though 4.75pt and 12pt were also used. These type sizes had names like ruby, pearl and minion. In fact, typography has its own distinct lexicon. Now we simply use the number — for example, 7pt. The body text in this book is set in 11pt New Century Schoolbook on 15pt leading.

Headlines were traditionally set in 14pt and 18pt, and then in 6pt increments up to 60pt. Occasionally 12pt was used as a

# 60pt Arial
# 54pt Arial
# 48pt Arial
# 42pt Arial
# 36pt Arial
# 30pt Arial
# 24pt Arial

**Figure 5.2: A range of headlines, ranging in 6pt increments.**

headline for fillers and briefs. After 60pt headlines increased by 12pt — that is 72pt or 84pt, and so on. Tabloid papers often run headlines in 84pt or 96pt, and some have been known to go up to 180pt.

With modern typesetting technology, it is possible to have headlines of any size. Some desktop publishing (DTP) systems such as QuarkXPress offer type sizes from 1pt through to 999pt, with increments of 0.001pt. This rubber form of type, you will agree, is probably overly generous — more on this scenario later. Obviously, the larger the type, the more space it occupies. Publishers and designers strike a balance between economics — striving to fit as much into the available number of pages — and legibility — making the product easy to read.

Twenty-five years ago, most Australasian newspapers set their body text in 7pt for news, and went as small as 5pt for sports results. Today this is considered too small, especially for people with poor or failing eyesight. Most Australasian and UK newspapers set their body type between 8pt and 9.5pt. Some American papers have increased body text to 9.8pt, with another half a point of leading, to accommodate older readers. More on reading and leading (pronounced 'ledding') later.

## The importance of x-height

In the chapter on headlines you will have noted that characters vary in size. Some such as the *m* and *w* are wide. Others like *i* and *l* are slim. Obviously choice of words matters when writing a headline. Most letters have a relatively consistent bowl size (see Figure 5.1) because type is designed to be aesthetically pleasing as well as functional. The x-height is the height of that character, but has come to mean the height of text without the ascenders or descenders.

In any font — that is an individual member of a type family or style — letters of the same point size have the same x-height. But the letters of one font may look very different compared with the letters of the same size in *another* font. Figure 5.3 on the next page shows that the a's are all the same type size — 24pt — but they come from different type families with different design objectives and have different x-heights. Thus they have different shapes.

a          a          a          a          a

**Figure 5.3: All the characters are 24pt but they vary in size because of their different x-heights. From left: Bookman, Garamond, Helvetica, New Century Schoolbook and Palatino.**

The x-height influences the ease with which people read a publication and the size in which body text is set. Newspapers have tended to choose type with a *large* x-height. These typefaces have correspondingly small ascenders and descenders because the larger the x-height the smaller the available space for the ascenders and descenders in a given point size. Typefaces with a large x-height are said to be 'big on the body'. Newspapers prefer them because their large bowls are less likely to fill with ink and blot out some characters on poor quality paper such as newsprint. Some mature-age readers will remember how the bowls of the letters on our old manual typewriter used to get caked with dirt and ink. You could argue that modern newspapers use better quality newsprint compared with, say, a generation ago. But it is still not high-quality paper and newspapers still tend to prefer body text that is 'big on the body'.

The other reason is economic. You can get away with using smaller size type if it has a large x-height. Type with a large x-height looks larger than the same size type with a small x-height. For example, 8pt Century will be just as easy to read as 9.5pt Bodoni (which has a small x-height and relatively long ascenders and descenders). This means you can generally get more words into the same space, depending on the design of the type. Of the literally hundreds of thousands of typefaces available, only a handful are used regularly for newspaper production. The deputy managing editor for graphics at *USA Today*, Ford Huffman, is quoted as recommending these typefaces for newspapers in an article for *Design*, the journal of the Society of News Design:

| | |
|---|---|
| Centennial | Janson |
| Century Old Style | Nimrod |
| Charter | Olympian |
| Corona | Plantin |
| Excelsior | Times |
| Gulliver | Utopia |

Type is also said to have varying weights. That is, the typeface can be printed in its standard, or Roman, form or in variations known as **bold**, *italic* and ***bold italic***. This issue is discussed further in the last section on headline typography.

## Serif versus sans serif type

Several other factors influence legibility and readability. One is the choice of serif or sans serif type. Type is *either* serif or sans serif. Serifs are the small extra bits on the ends of letters. Sans type (sans comes from the French, meaning 'without') generally has a simpler design. The two phrases below in Figure 5.4 show the differences between a 24pt serif type on the left (Times) and a 24pt sans serif type (Geneva).

# type hype      type hype

**Figure 5.4: Differences between 24pt serif Times on the left and a 24pt sans serif Geneva.**

Some historians say the serifs began as embellishments chiselled on letters by Roman craftsmen; hence the term 'Roman' that describes the standard version of typefaces. Other researchers say serifs were imitations of the flourishes that scribes made with quill pens when they transcribed books. Most books were hand-copied before Johann Gutenberg's invention of moveable type in Germany in the mid-fifteenth century. Others say serifs were used to prevent cracks in the stone or wood on which type was mounted. Cracks tend to follow the grain of the material used, so serifs were cut at angles to the vertical or horizontal, to reduce stress on the material. Remember that, before computerized typesetting, type was carved from blocks of wood and later set in lead. Type had to be strong to withstand the punishing processes of page assembly and printing.

Serif type is easier to read in body text. Most newspapers prefer it because, in 8pt or 9pt, its 'tops and tails' are better defined than the 'straight lines' of sans serif type. Some of the most readable faces — New Century Schoolbook, Bookman and Caslon Book — were originally designed for books. These are also excellent newspaper faces, though they tend to gobble up space. But there is another reason for the popularity of serif typefaces linked with how we read.

## A short lesson on how we read

We read by scanning text line by line, left to right. Your eyes do not move smoothly. They move anywhere from one to three centimetres and pause for a fraction of a second. These pauses are called fixations. We absorb information during the fixations, not during the scan. We learn to read by recognizing the shapes of words. Each word has an individual template or shape. Serifs help the eyes join letters and words. Serifs also give each word an individual shape, as you will see in Figure 5.5 below. You will notice that the serif type has the most *unique* shape, while the capitals have a block-like shape. Because the serif word shape is unique, it is easier to recognize and remember. Subs notice literals, incidentally, because the shape of the mis-spelled word clashes with the shape in our memory.

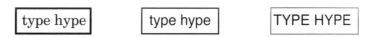

**Figure 5.5: Serif type gives words an individual shape. Note that capitals offer the least unique template.**

Research about word shape and reading explains why it is best to use lower case type for body text. Words in capitals are difficult to read because their shapes are so regular. They can easily be confused with other similar shapes. As a general rule, never set body type in capitals — though they are useful for EMPHASIS. And, even then, never set more than a few words in capitals. They take up about 30 per cent more space, compared with the same number of words in lower case. When we read, we deduce meaning from the shape of words and phrases, along with the context and our past knowledge. Serif type helps readers recognize shapes. US research shows that people read serif type about seven or eight per cent faster than sans.

Serif type is also more legible on newspapers with long print runs. Characters remain easier to read despite the use of thin inks and relatively poor-quality newsprint. The only exception applies to reverse type — white type on a dark background. You should never set serif type in reverse if it is under 12pt because the serifs get lost in the background darkness. Always use sans serif type for small reverses. Sans also reads more easily in the tiny sizes — under 7pt.

# Finding optimum column width

As a general rule, the best size for body text is somewhere between 8pt and 9.5pt, depending on the x-height and the amount of leading (the vertical space per line). We will discuss leading later. Body type needs to be large because type smaller than 8pt is difficult to read, even for people with good eyesight. The older a paper's readership, the bigger the body type needs to be. For example, body text should be set in 9.5pt. World Health Organization figures show that just over 60 per cent of people among the western nations do not have perfect eyesight. Typographers and designers should conduct a comprehensive survey to find out about their audience. It is pointless designing a great 'look' for a paper for people who cannot physically read it. The optimum column width also depends on the size of the body text selected, which is directly related to the type's x-height. Here is a simple formula for calculating the optimum width. Set one and a half alphabet lengths of the body type you intend to use. An alphabet length is the 26 lower case characters set next to each other, without spaces, so one and a half alphabet lengths would be 39 characters. For example, one and a half alphabet lengths for 10pt Palatino would look like this:

abcdefghijklmnopqrstuvwxyzabcdefghijklm

**Figure 5.6: 10pt Palatino set on one and a half alphabet lengths.**

To find the optimum column width, all you have to do is measure the horizontal distance with your em rule. The width of a column is measured in pica ems. This is usually abbreviated to ems in England, New Zealand and Australia. In the US they are called picas. Historically, pica was the printer's term for 12pt type. The term 'em' comes from the letter m because it and w are the widest letters in the alphabet.

---

1. One and a half alphabet lengths for 9pt Times New Roman, shown below, gives an optimum width of 14.5 ems.

   abcdefghijklmnopqrstuvwxyzabcdefghijklm

2. One and a half alphabet lengths for 9pt Bookman, shown below, provides an optimum width of 16.5 ems.

   abcdefghijklmnopqrstuvwxyzabcdefghijklm

3. One and a half alphabet lengths for 9pt New Century Schoolbook, shown below, gives an optimum column width of 15.5 ems.

   Abcdefghijklmnopqrstuvwxyzabcdefghijklm

---

**Figure 5.7: Examples of one and a half alphabet lengths of different typefaces. Different faces give different widths.**

The examples in Figure 5.7 show why Times is such a popular font for newspapers around the English-speaking world. It
occupies the least amount of space of any typeface, yet remains
extremely legible. Do a similar calculation for the body type of
your newspaper. Are the columns narrower than the optimum
width? To accommodate advertisers' needs, broadsheet papers
have traditionally had somewhere between 10 and 12 columns,
while tabloids have worked on eight to 10 column grids. The
next chapter on design suggests that designers should stick
with a consistent number of columns throughout the paper.
Assuming a body text of, say, 9pt then the ideal number of
columns for an Australian or English broadsheet should be
about seven. For a tabloid, it should be about five.

US broadsheets have adopted a narrower printing width to
save paper — 25 inches across both pages (or just over 34 cm
for a single page) — so the optimum number of columns should
be somewhere between five and six. *The New York Times*, for
example, has adopted a consistent six-column grid for all editorial content. Many tabloid papers prefer to vary column width
for each page, often each story, to present a lively appearance.

# Styles of typesetting

Type can be set justified or unjustified. With justified type,
the text is artificially spaced out to the left and right column
margins to give a uniform look to the paragraph. Text in the
news sections of newspapers is almost always justified.
Almost all of the paragraphs in this book are justified. Justified setting comes in two styles:

1. justified and hyphenated
2. justified and unhyphenated

## Justified and hyphenated

Text in the news sections of most newspapers is justified and hyphenated (hence

the h&j button on your terminal). This paragraph is set over 17.5 ems. Hyphenation saves space by breaking words sensibly, which reduces the likelihood of rivers of white space running through the text. Hyphenation is vital for narrow columns — under 8 ems. It is best to avoid more than three hyphens in a row.

## Justified and unhyphenated

With this setting style words are not hyphenated so bigger spaces are forced between the words to maintain a uniform column width. This method can look neat and tidy.

But it looks absolutely awful with narrow columns (anything under eight ems) because you get massive rivers of white between words, especially when the text contains abundant polysyllabic words.

However, justified and unhyphenated text can look good on wide columns (say, 22–30 ems). If you do not hyphenate text, you *waste* valuable space. The body text in most newspapers is justified and hyphenated to fit as much text in as possible. For variety and to give a 'softer' look, some sections or stories are set 'ragged right' and 'ragged left' (see below and on the next page).

## Ragged right

This unjustified style is used to good effect in feature sections in quality British newspapers like *The Guardian*. The ragged right look is believed to give the feature sections a distinct personality and to make them look different from news sections, which are almost always hyphenated and justified.

## Ragged left

This method is known as ragged left because the text is aligned against the right margin and the left edge is, well, ragged. The orderly impression given by justified type suits the image of news columns. The more informal and less precise nature of ragged right is appropriate for feature material. But most designers tend to use ragged left setting sparingly. As you are beginning to notice, it gets difficult to read because the eye returns automatically to the left margin to start a new line. With ragged left setting there is no consistent start point and the eye is bounced around. Notice how difficult this was to read, compared with the flush left text.

## Leading

Another technical term mentioned earlier is leading. The term comes from hot-metal days when compositors filled stories that fell short by inserting slivers of lead between lines of text. Leading is used nowadays for design reasons, to make text easier to read. A font with a large x-height needs more leading than another type of the same size with a small x-height. Extra leading — usually half a point in modern newspapers — puts parallel slabs of white space between lines, helping the eyes flow more freely from one line to another. Type with a large x-height that is set across a wide measure (more than 25 ems) needs extra leading — a full point is best.

As a general guide, condensed typefaces need about 1pt of leading in larger sizes (12–14pt) but half to a quarter a point is enough for the smaller sizes (10pt and under). This is a classic example of the conflict between economy and design. With modern typesetting systems it is easy for subs to insert leading electronically. Page designers need to experiment to find the ideal leading for a particular typeface and size. Remember that leading should be used to enhance reading, not just to fill space when copy falls short, though deadlines will sometimes see this rule bent. Times has long been popular as a body text because it requires minimal leading. Stanley Morison designed it for *The Times* of London and it was first used in 1932. The more leading you add, the less space you have for words.

# Kerning and condensing headlines

Kerning involves decreasing the spaces between letters. Its original purpose was to make words easier to read by removing the excess between certain letters. Notice the space between the two sans serif letters in Figure 5.8 below, especially when we move to a larger size, as in these examples of 24pt Geneva:

**Figure 5.8: An example of unkerned (left) and kerned (right) text.**

Intelligent kerning increases legibility. Most typesetting software allows you to set kerning tables. Often they are built into newspaper front-end systems. Kerning has subsequently become a way to make headlines fit when they are slightly too big. Most papers sensibly adopt policies that limit the amount of headline kerning. The factor that decides by how much should be the typeface itself.

Some faces like Helvetica respond well to kerning. Others, particularly serifs with big flourishes and some thin sans serif characters, do not because kerning will simply make characters run into each other, like melted chocolate. See Figure 5.9 on the next page for an example.

# A headline like melted chocolate

**Figure 5.9: An example of a headline with too much kerning.**

Condensing is the squeezing of letters from the sides to make them thinner — it is a bit like putting a corset on the headline. It is another way to get a headline to fit. Again, most publications limit the amount of condensing. The Cybergraphic system allows you to use a command 'lw' (line width) followed by a minus and a number. This condenses the headline by a specific proportion or percentage based on the number. At many publications the maximum 'lw' command is minus 3, or 10 per cent.

Certain typefaces are already condensed. Others are extra condensed. Examples are Record Gothic Extra Condensed and Gill Sans Bold Condensed. Type designers also deliberately widen letters and these faces are said to be extended. Some examples include Record Bold Extended and Helvetica Black Extended.

## Musings on headline typography

Because headlines are read differently to body text, it does not matter whether you use serif or sans serif fonts. Each style has moved in and out of fashion over the years. The letters in headlines occupy so much space, relative to the short span of the eye during reading, that reading theory does not apply. For years, purists have argued that designers should never mix sans heads with serif body type, and vice versa. Today, designers are free to choose but some general rules can be applied to headline typography. Headlines need to be clean, appropriate and economical. By clean, I mean they should be uncluttered: that is, choose a typeface that is devoid of swirls and swashes, and loops and ligatures, not to mention tails and terminals. Headline type should also be appropriate for the story. You would not, for example, use a huge bold condensed sans headline for a story about a romantic wedding; you would not put a 60pt bold caps head on a two-paragraph filler. By economical, I mean the face should produce enough characters over a standard single column to make it relatively easy to write a headline. It is frustrating and difficult to write a good head if you have, say, only four characters over a single column.

Your paper should also have enough 'weight' variations of a type family to provide you with **bold**, *italic* and ***bold italic*** versions. Figure 5.10 below is an example of a range of headline weights in 24pt Times.

$$\textit{Times italic}$$
$$\textbf{Times bold}$$
$$\textbf{\textit{Times bold italic}}$$

**Figure 5.10: An example of various weights of 24pt Times.**

I hope you never encounter the problem I once had on a provincial paper during hot-metal days. The paper had a limited range of letters for display type. The main front page lead always had three decks of 72pt caps over four columns (40 ems). Headlines had to be written with no more than two E's because that is all they had. Try writing a three-deck headline, with a maximum of 10 or 11 characters in each deck, using only two E's.

Now that you know something about typography, it is time to proceed to the next chapter on design. Hopefully you can appreciate that an understanding of typography is a foundation for good design and legibility. The getting of wisdom is said to be an appreciation of how little we know about anything. With time, you will find that the more you know about typography, the more you will want to know.

# Exercises

1. Ask a magazine or newspaper designer for their thoughts on the influence of typography on their work. Write a 400-word feature on the influence of typography on publication design.

2. Study the typography of a newspaper or magazine that you admire or hate. List 10 ways in which the use of type enhances (or gets in the way of) your enjoyment of that publication.

3. Calculate the optimum column width for the body type of your newspaper.

# References

Evans, Harold (1974). *Editing & Design* (Book Three — *News headlines*). London: Heinemann. See Chapter 5.

Giles, Vic & Hodgson, F.W. (1990). *Creative Newspaper Design*. London: Heinemann. See Chapter 2.

Harrower, Tim (1999). *The Newspaper Designer's Handbook*. Fourth edition. William Brown.

Hutt, Allen & James, Bob (1989). *Newspaper Design Today*. London: Lund Humphries. See pages 23–33.

*Design*, the journal of the Society of News Design, Summer 2000. See pages 9–10.

# 6 The art and craft of publication design

## Summary

- Newspapers: A visual medium
- A design process
- Formulating a design policy
- The need for visual literacy
- Produce a written design policy
- Choose appropriate typography
- The key design elements
- Image selection and position
- Modular design
- How to simplify design
- A recommended procedure for designing a page

GOOD design is a publication's best advertisement for itself. The design might look restrained, authoritative, lively, even sensational — but it should never look ordinary. Fashions come and go, but quality always succeeds. Apologies for the cliché but sometimes clichés are apt. How do we achieve quality? By sticking to good design principles, and remembering that we are in the information and communication business. Design is about making information accessible. Designers should aim to make navigation as easy as possible for the reader.

Before we proceed let us take a small diversion into the land of analogy. Analogies are sometimes useful. Good design is like preparing a bowl of soup. Essentially we mix ingredients to produce something we hope will appeal to our readers' palates. News executives choose the ingredients (also known as content) and select what will go where in the same way that a good cook selects ingredients. They taste copy to decide what to use. They smell out a page lead. And they know that as with any dish, presentation — how it looks — is as important as how it tastes.

On daily newspapers the news editor does the selecting; on non-daily papers it is often the editor. On magazines the editor usually chairs a small committee. The food analogy also applies to the context. To explain, let us go back to the soup. Soup is contained in a bowl; it is the context which holds the content (the liquid). Hopefully the analogy is not too souperficial. For the designer or sub-editor, design policy and knowledge of the publication's perceived audience provides the context. All well-designed publications are produced for a perceived audience. Intelligent publications conduct research to find out who that audience is.

# Newspapers: A visual medium

The deputy managing editor for graphics with *USA Today*, Ford Huffman, summarized the theme of this chapter when he said that many newspapers in the late twentieth century still did not understand that newspapers are a visual medium in a visual and global world. 'Most newspapers still cling to the belief that if we run it, they will read it. Not so.'

He noted research from the Poynter Institute that showed readers look at a quarter of the text on a page and read about half of that. 'Yet we still put out many newspapers that rely on narrative paragraphs to tell stories, paragraphs full of numerals and percentages. And often the very paragraphs we use are unreadable because of typeface choices and awkward wordspacing.' It is time for editors to realize that visual elements improve newspapers. We are, after all, in the communication business.

# A design process

This chapter will consider a process for designing news publications. The process can be summarized thus:

- Formulate a design policy that is appropriate for your audience
- Choose appropriate typography
- Use the key elements of text, visuals and white space
- Introduce new communication methods such as 'infographics'

# Formulating a design policy

Designers and subs should formulate a design policy based on a combination of what their audience wants and needs, plus what journalists believe they should have. So the process should always start with: 'Who are you designing for?' If you do not know, find out. Once you are aware of your audience — and have sorted out an appropriate design policy — it is relatively easy to write appropriate headlines, choose appropriate illustrations and produce appropriate design. A design theory based on knowledge of the audience helps designers and subs do their job better.

Finally — and this is as far as I will stretch the soup analogy — when eating soup we need a spoon. This tool makes the job so much easier. In publication design terms, the main tool is pagination. Most magazines and newspapers have converted to some form of pagination. Magazines use Macintosh hardware and DTP software. Most daily papers also employ specialized pagination products. The most common in the late twentieth century were Atex with the Press2Go QuarkXPress extensions, Cybergraphic and Systems Integrators International (SII). More recently, Windows and Unix-based products have become available.

Designers and sub-editors must know how to design on screen. This chapter introduces the principles for designing print publications, and shows how to apply them.

## Know your reader

All readers have needs, but these needs vary. You need to define your audience. There are many ways to do so. The advertising industry uses demographic and psychographic methods. You can borrow from them. Audience research people use surveys. Subs should be free to pillage their results. American newspapers use research or focus groups of readers who come to the paper every few months to provide feedback. You can develop mini versions of these. Designers need an audience profile. The most successful publication launches have been based on extensive audience research. Build prototypes based on your research. Provide lots of variations. Show them to lots of people and get lots of feedback. It is time-consuming but worth the effort.

Once you have established who you are talking to, you can instigate a design policy. Everything should flow from that policy. One useful tip is to read publications that cater for a similar audience. When producing a prototype of a new publication, it is helpful to show it to that audience. It is vital to have a clear picture of what you intend to do. Summarize your audience profile in a couple of sentences. Because you are catering for an audience, the key word for content must be 'relevant'. The more relevant the articles, photos, graphs and cartoons are for your audience, the more chance you have of holding their attention and loyalty.

# The need for visual literacy

Most magazines and some daily papers employ graphic designers. Many non-daily papers assign the job to sub-editors. To do the job well requires a high level of visual literacy, something that people with a text background often do not possess. They need to acquire it. Usually this happens on the job, but sometimes editors acquire it via tertiary study. Ideally all employers should offer in-house training in visual literacy. In mid 2000, the president of the Society for News Design in the United States, Jean Moxam Dodd, called for higher standards of visual literacy among designers, along with improvements in visual journalism education at universities and continued training for people in the industry.

Designer Tim Harrower, who has written the best book to date on newspaper design, points out that newspapers are competing with television and the Web in terms of visual appeal. 'Have they [designers and editors] noticed how slick graphics are on TV? In books? On Web sites? Newspapers, in truth, are the bottom feeders in the great food chain of design.'

The former president of the Society for News Design, Ed Kohorst, believes visual journalists have yet to achieve parity with text journalists. 'The culture of most news rooms still recognizes a tradition that suspects creativity and tolerates visuals as a necessary evil.'

In Australia, a former regional director of the Society for News Design, Peter Ong, maintains that newspapers are giving higher visibility and emphasis to visual journalism. 'But one thing that sorely needs serious research is the question of words vis-à-vis visuals. Does it mean that with more emphasis on the visual side of journalism, there will be fewer words? Or are newspapers just giving more space to visuals without a corresponding reduction in words?'

# Produce a written design policy

Design strategy or policy should exist on paper, either as a printed style book or an electronic file. Keep it simple initially. You can always get more complicated later. Be consistent. Design policy should have one main purpose — to help readers find information easily, and to help them absorb it easily once they get there. A publication that is easy to read sells better than one that is difficult to read. This particularly applies when catering for the television age. People raised on a diet of television, video, cinema, advertising and the like are visually mature. They expect visual presentations to be sophisticated and they expect them to be easy to absorb. TV, video and cinema do the work for the viewer. In a way, as a designer you also have to work for the reader.

Time is also important. People are busy. We still have the same amount of time in a day and we generally still sleep the same number of hours, but we have more things to do. A major reason people give for cancelling a newspaper subscription, especially Monday to Friday, is their perception that they are wasting their money because they do not have time to read the paper.

For the same reason, readership of weekend papers has generally risen worldwide. People have more free time at weekends. Research suggests that people spend an average of about 20 to 30 minutes a day reading a paper during the week. Readers want regular sections to be in the same place so they know where to find them. Designers have a major role in their publication's future. How you design a publication is as important as what goes into it.

# Choose appropriate typography

Appropriate typography should be part of design policy. Designers and editors need to understand typography — the study of type — and its influence on legibility and readability. Select fonts that are appropriate for your audience.

Choose the best headline fonts you have — preferably no more than two — and concentrate on them. For contrast, use them in the italic, bold or bold italic versions of the same face. Pick fonts that 'marry' well with each other. Also consider that font's potential to be kerned, because some faces look terrible when they are squeezed. If you need to, review the previous chapter on typography.

# The key design elements

Designers get to play with three basic elements. Success as a designer depends on your ability to combine them. Those three elements are:

■ text

■ visuals

■ white space

The first two terms are obvious. By text I mean all the words in the publication — the body type, headlines, summary heads, captions, bylines, the publication's flag and masthead, the continue lines, the sub-heads and cross-heads, and the break-out quotes. That is why typography has been emphasized. By visuals I mean all the visual elements: the photographs, cartoons, graphs, charts, illustrations and 'infographics'. Visuals are dealt with in the next two chapters.

The third term is perhaps not so obvious. By white space I mean the context that holds the content of text and image. It is what surrounds the first two elements and shapes the design. A publication's design strategy or policy is reflected in the way you use white space. In some respects it is what separates one publication from another in terms of how people see it. It is part of what makes the look of *The Guardian* radically different from the *Daily Telegraph* in the UK. It helps make *USA Today* stand apart from *The New York Times*. It is one of the reasons the *Courier-Mail* in Brisbane does not resemble *The Age* in Melbourne in Australia.

## White space

The first two elements — text and visuals — are tangible. They can be moved around the page, and manipulated in the sense of being enlarged or reduced. They are the page content. White space — the landscape on which you arrange the text and images — is the complementary third element. Remember the soup bowl at the start of the chapter? White space provides the context. It is easy enough to throw text and image together, but the results can look dreadful.

Creativity becomes involved in the way you combine text and visuals with white space. Two aspects of space need to be considered: external constraints and design space. By the former I mean how much or how little space you have to work with. With newspapers the issue is usually how little space is available after advertisements have been positioned. The danger with insufficient space is the urge to jam too much in. Think about your readers and resist that urge. In the other aspect, design space provides the pattern or shape for the page. It is a difficult concept to express in words. It is not the area left over after the important text and images have been inserted. It is also not the no-man's land between text and headline, or body text and gutter. It is easier to demonstrate with an example. A classic version is a full-page advertisement with nothing more than a 10 cm box of text centred on the page. The acres of blank space draw the reader's eyes to the text. Think of white space as a frame around pages and elements on those pages.

As a general rule, the more white space around a group of elements than between them will group those elements together. Similarly, the more space between elements pushes them apart. Figure 6.1 illustrates this concept.

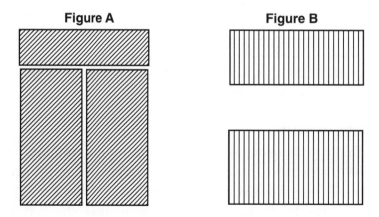

**Figure 6.1: In Figure A at left, more white space around the three elements than between them brings the elements together. The reverse applies in Figure B at right.**

Among other things, white space is used to:

- draw the reader's eye to a particular area or subject
- provide an overall theme or shape to an article
- make reading a publication easier
- give readers' eyes a rest from masses of grey body text

White space gives clarity and direction to a page. It works effectively if it has a clearly defined geometric shape. In magazines, for example, it can be used to tie successive pages together through repeating the same shape. Similarly, magazines and books have wide margins that subconsciously suggest the publication will be easy to read. Newspapers provide consistent column width and gutters between columns to give the reader the impression the publication is ordered and easy to approach. Intelligent use of leading is another example of using white space to make reading more pleasant. Refer to the previous chapter on typography for recommendations on leading.

Think of white space as a juggling act between getting all the information you require on to a page, and ensuring the information is presented so it easy for the reader to comprehend. It may be a case of trial and error, but eventually you will get a feel for its appropriate use. Newspaper designers cannot always be generous with white space. But they can develop a feel for the best way to use white space to enhance design. Sometimes the best place to experiment is on the features pages, where you generally have more time to play.

# Image selection and position

Research from several parts of the world shows that for print publications, **pictures and large headlines attract substantially more attention than text** when people encounter a page. With words, the brain has to decipher the abstract order of the letters. Pictures and headlines are absorbed much more as a whole. (It is interesting that the latter is known as 'display type', which shows that large headlines have two roles. The words perform literary and visual functions.) When designing a page, place large images first — anything bigger than three columns. This image is known as the centre of visual impact, or CIV, and it is discussed in the next couple of pages. The role, relevance and importance of images to design is elaborated upon in the next chapter.

## The designer's role

Designers should make content as accessible as possible. Given that most readers have limited time, your job as a page designer is to make reading as easy as possible as you direct people around the page. You should assume that the reader's interest is pretty superficial, and that it is your job to manage it. When people pick up a newspaper or magazine, some tend to browse the page the way a cow meanders around a field. Copious research has been done on how people look at a page. Some researchers say that with broadsheet pages, the eye goes from top left to bottom right, meandering through the centre. Others say readers tend to start somewhere in the centre and lock on to anything that holds their interest (the CVI). Much of the research is inconclusive. At best we can accept that people read from left to right, and move down a page from top to bottom. They have a consistent destination — the 'exit' at the bottom right.

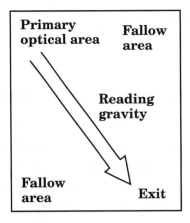

**Figure 6.2: Edmund Arnold's Gutenberg diagram.**

American typographer Edmund Arnold devised the Gutenberg diagram to explain this concept in the early 1950s. Pretty much all research on how people read agrees on this point — they all end up at the exit point. Arnold calls this tendency to travel down the page 'reading gravity'. His diagram suggests that because of reading gravity the eye tends to miss the top right and bottom left of any page. He calls them 'fallow areas'. Arnold calls the top left-hand corner the primary optical area because he believes this is where people start. Figure 6.2 shows the Gutenberg diagram.

## Eyetrack research for print design

Chapter 9 discusses new research that Stanford University and the Poynter Institute conducted to find how people read online news sites. In the late 1980s the Gallup Organization did similar studies on how people read newspapers. It involved placing small cameras on a people's heads. The cameras tracked how people's eyes moved as they browsed pages. *Presstime*, the magazine of the Newspaper Association of America, reported some of the more interesting findings. One was the high percentage of people who read headlines. 'The readership of stories dropped off to 30 to 50 per cent if the headline didn't seem to promise an interesting story,' staff writer Gene Goltz noted.

The research also showed that people responded to photographs. More people spent more time on headlines and photographs than any other elements. The same research conducted in non English-speaking countries produced similar results, leading to the reasonable generalization that newspaper readers look first at display heads and large images.

### Gutenberg versus capturing the reader's eye

Designer Phil Nesbitt believes that the designer controls where the reader goes through judicious use of images and headlines. Nesbitt argues that the Gutenberg diagram works on a blank page, but the designer can decide where people's eyes go by using display elements intelligently and appropriately. The designer 'determines where the reader goes on the page', Nesbitt says. A compelling photograph will create a different primary optical area wherever you place that image. Elements on a page act as guideposts, 'leading readers through the page in the hope that they will cover as much of the page as possible'. In effect, the designer's job is to make life as easy as possible for the reader. How do we do this? Nesbitt maintains that readers subconsciously prioritize elements on a page. He lists them in descending order of visual impact with the most powerful first.

■ Strong (and large) photographs

■ Graphics

■ Eye-catching, bold headlines

■ Large and unusual type

■ Separate colour elements such as reverses and tints

■ White space

■ Rules and borders

■ Body text

Photographs and graphics are discussed in the next two chapters. Another factor that needs to be included in this list is modular design. Let us discuss the elements in Nesbitt's hierarchy.


## Headline size and position

Headlines should indicate what the publication considers the most important stories on the page. The bigger the head, the more important the story. Heads should decrease proportionately as you go down the page. Traditionally the reduction has been in 6pt or 12pt jumps. Thus the heads on a broadsheet page might start at 60pt, then decrease to 48pt, then 42pt, then 36pt. Tabloids work the same way, though some scream louder with larger display type.

Technology allows subs to kern and squeeze headlines, so the reductions tend to be less traditional on modern newspapers. But it is still important to be consistent and to limit the percentage of kerning that any headline must endure.

Editors can also use different weights to indicate story importance, and to achieve contrast. Thus your lead headline could be in bold, with other headlines Roman or italic — though all should be from the same type family. With a picture story, where the image occupies more than three columns, always place the headline **below** the picture and caption, and above the body text. Why? Because most readers go to the picture first and then look for the caption below — effectively ignoring the headline that the sub has spent time crafting.

### Headline shape

Shapes are covered in Chapter 3. Newspapers have mostly adopted centred or flush left heads. Centred heads can look good either long-short-long or long-medium-long. But short-long-short should be avoided — it looks dreadful. Flush left heads are common on news pages. They look good if you include a one em or en indent that leaves more white space on the page. Some designers like to set news headlines left and centre the heads on feature pages. I prefer flush left heads for news and features, always with an en indent. They tend to be easier to write.

## Typographical design elements

Typographical tricks can be used to enhance page design. They break up text to make stories more readable and visually appealing. Some of the more useful methods, in no specific order of merit, are:

- First word caps
- Drop or initial caps
- Key words
- Tones and tints
- Blobs and stars
- Boxes and rules

### FIRST word caps

THIS device draws attention to the first word, as in this paragraph. It is common in the USA, England and Europe, and some of the better-looking Australian newspapers. Introductions should be written so the key words are as close as possible to the start of the sentence. This requires a new attitude among reporters and subs to writing intros — no more ponderous sentences that take 10 words just to describe the person or organization speaking: The president of the Australian League of Decency towards Donkeys, Dr Daniel Dibbs, today decried what he described as the increasing tendency towards . . . The English popular tabloids use this first-word technique brilliantly. This example is fiction but hopefully it makes the point:

## Vicar in court

RANDY vicar Myron Splurt, 35, admitted in Blanksville District Court yesterday that he had group sex with three member of his congregation at a party last year.

### Drop caps and initial caps

**D**rop caps fall into the text, as this example shows. Though originally a display method in feature articles, they are moving into news sections. *The Guardian*, for example, has showed a preference for them over the years.

**I**nitial caps stick above the line of text, and are mostly used in feature stories, often to break up body text. Usually the first word, and sometimes the first line, are set in capitals, as this paragraph shows.

MAGAZINES LIKE *ROLLING STONE* CAPITALIZE THE first line of the first column; other magazines have a style that requires, say, the first five lines to be set in capitals. Some look better than others. It is your choice. Just remember that you are designing to help readers, not to impress art school graduates or your colleagues and friends at other publications.

## Key words

Tabloid English papers used to highlight words or paragraphs in body text by putting them in CAPITALS, or **bold**, or *italic*, or ***ANY*** combination of these weights. It was a popular method for emphasis and capturing the reader's eye in the 1980s. But it was overdone and some designers stopped using them. Generally bold is better than italic for **emphasis** because some publications use italic for the names of books, newspapers and foreign phrases. Do not abuse the idea of key words through overuse.

## Tones, tints and reverses

If you must use tones, tints and reverses, use them rarely. With modern production systems it takes only a few seconds to put a 10 per cent or 20 per cent tint under a box. Never go higher than 20 per cent — text becomes too difficult to read. Always use bold type over a tint. Reverses — white text on a black background, sometimes known as a WOB — are excellent design enhancements, provided they are used sparingly.

> Reversed text smaller than 12pt should always be sans serif; otherwise the serifs get lost in the dark background, as this line of 8pt Century Schoolbook shows.

## Blobs and stars

These should also be used sparingly and intelligently. They are an excellent way to:

◆ highlight key points and

▲ break up a mass of grey text.

Used badly, they can make a page very confusing because the reader's eye is attracted by too many points of interest. Apply the same rule for blobs and stars as you would with swear words — they are much more effective when used sparingly and in the right place.

The same can be said of sub-heads and cross-heads. In the days of hot-metal production, printers and subs used to add them to fill gaps when copy fell short. It should not happen with new technology because there are easier ways to fill gaps, such as inserting extra leading or a single-column photograph, or increasing the body text size by 0.1 of a point. The method you choose will depend on available time and the size of the gap to be filled. One reason that sub-heads and cross-heads have fallen out of favour is the belief that time-poor readers will use them as ways to escape a story. That is, they will read only as far as the first sub-head and then leave.

## Boxes and rules

Boxes help bring the eye to a particular part of the page, such as a story you want to highlight. For example, you might want to highlight a list of petrol prices linked to a longer story about a

> Remember to ensure a gap of two to three characters between text and box. Otherwise the text crashes into the box and becomes difficult to read. Boxes are also suitable for highlighting a regular column or opinion piece. Generally they should be used sparingly, to highlight something worthwhile. Rules should be used discreetly and sensibly.

petrol price-cutting war and its effect on the economy. You could box the whole item with a 1pt rule and put a hairline rule around the price list. Or you could position the price list in its own box somewhere conspicuous inside the main story, or use the list the same way you would a single-column photo or break-out quote. Avoid vertical rules between columns. Horizontal rules lead the eye across the page. They need to be bold to differentiate individual stories, especially in horizontal modular layout.

# Modular design

In the past decade, almost all newspapers in Europe (the UK in particular), Australasia and the United States have adopted modular design. With this approach, the designer works in rectangular blocks. Dog-legs and other asymmetrical shapes are avoided. Modular design has numerous advantages. It is clean and looks neat. It is popular with readers because they perceive it as easy to read. It is popular with publishers and editorial executives because it means that all staff quickly become familiar with standard page templates. It is also locked in as a feature in most front-end production systems, which would partly explain its popularity.

Modular design forces newspapers to be better organized. Its only disadvantage is the need sometimes to cut or pad stories unnecessarily to fit a pre-ordained news hole. Careful planning avoids this problem, as does training reporters to write to a specific length. Pages can be designed to accommodate a story that is too good to cut. Photographs can be positioned early to their best advantage and text and headlines allocated later. A well-designed page should not need fillers. If you have small stories you plan to highlight, put them in a section for news in brief (NIB). Figure 6.3 on the next page shows the main elements that make up a page. Note that it is a modular design.

# How to simplify design

The associate director of the American Press Institute, Warren Watson, has proposed ways to simplify design to allow more time for reporting and editing. He suggests news publications should adopt format layouts. These are standardized pages where each day the same position is allocated for the lead photograph and lead story, and stories are flowed into pre-designated spaces.

Allied with this should be a grid system. *The New York Times*, for example, has chosen a six-column format that is consistent throughout the paper. Watson also suggests papers should develop schedules for headline and image sizes. The *Geelong Advertiser* in Australia has a design policy built into its front-end system that specifies the range of sizes for headlines on specific pages. Subs can refer to these guidelines when building pages. Watson also urges papers to work around a centre of visual impact for each page. Reduce the number of stories that jump to other pages and employ modular design for editorial and advertisements. For the latter, square off advertisement stacks at the bottom of pages to allow more regular shape for editorial above. Finally, he recommends that designers practise 'whole' journalism.

A former editor of the *St Petersburg Times* in Florida, Gene Patterson, describes this as combining words, illustrations and page design as one entity to be 'handled whole'. It means creating a package that contains an enticing headline, a compelling photograph, energetic writing, a caption that goes beyond the obvious and engaging layout all in one package. A former editor of *US News and World Report*, Edwin Taylor, says

**Figure 6.3: The main elements that make up a page.**
Image courtesy of the Pacific Area Newspaper Publishers' Association.

designers should always be thinking of the reader or potential reader. 'Seeing the complete picture will allow the reader to make good progress, from element to element, before she or he has even started into the text.'

# A recommended procedure for designing a page

Here is a simple procedure for putting a page together. Ideally, assemble all of your material and then decide which is your main image — the centre of visual impact, or CVI — and your lead story. This is an idealized scenario because with daily newspapers it is not always possible to have everything ready. Sometimes subs are told to expect a photograph or story and they have to hope it will appear when it is supposed to appear. In this situation it is important to talk to the right people so that you know what you can expect, and when you can expect it. Get assurances that the stories and images you have made space for will arrive on time. If you have doubts, then arrange stand-bys.

Let us assume you have all your material. Read all the stories and get an accurate idea of how much space they will occupy and how much needs to be trimmed. You must know which stories are tightly written and difficult to trim and which ones can be cut easily. Decide on your page lead and how you plan to order the other stories in your list. Choose your best image. It is essential to know what advertisements will look like. If possible, get proofs of all advertisements next to editorial copy. A large advertisement with a heavy reverse or text in 84pt capitals can ruin a good photograph. Crop all your pictures tightly to show their best features.

## Place your strongest image first

Place your strongest image on the page first, using that image's most appropriate shape, and arrange the design around it. Trying to cram an image into the wrong shape after you have positioned all your text (a horizontal into a vertical, for example) produces awful design. Position your best image above the fold; that is, in the top half of the page. Broadsheet papers are folded when displayed on news-stands, and only the top half is visible. For that reason, broadsheets display their best image and headline to sell the paper to people buying from a news-stand. Some people sketch their ideas on a layout sheet before putting the page together. With practice, subs can design straight on to the screen. The rest of us mere mortals will continue to scribble on paper layout sheets. Thank goodness for erasers. Design your page from the top down. Ensure your headlines decrease in size as they go down the page, and use headline size to tell readers which stories you consider important. If you are new to page design it helps to devise a checklist, to ensure you cover all bases.

## Follow design policy

Follow your publication's design philosophy. If it advocates horizontal design, then stick with it. But also include the occasional long vertical to break up the 'same-ness' of this form. Horizontal layout makes writing headlines easier because it allows a greater flow of words. That is, one deck of horizontal text over four columns will permit more variety and number of words than four decks of single column text.

Pagination systems effectively force you to use modular design, so each story receives its own news hole. Avoid putting two double-column stories next to each other — they look awful. If you use single-column pictures or include break-out quotes, put them at the top of columns of text rather than in the middle. If you must place them in the middle of text, one option is to set the image or quote between columns, but make sure you do not get narrow lines of text on each side of the image with wide gaps between words.

Lift-out quotes, single column pictures and other forms of graphics provide visual relief. Readers love a news digest and/or an index on the front page. Surveys of what people read consistently show that these are very popular. Study well-designed newspapers and magazines to cherrypick ideas.

Sunday newspapers are often innovative because they have more time than daily papers.

In 1999, five people judged the world's best designed newspapers. From 321 entries from 29 countries they chose 39 finalists, then whittled those down to three. These were *Die Zeit* and *Die Woche*, both from Hamburg in Germany, and *Mural* from Zapopan in Mexico. The summer 2000 edition of *Design*, the journal of the Society for News Design, offers a pictorial spread of the winners and finalists. The judges' recommendations for improving papers are summarized here:

■ Reduce the information overload. Readers do not have time to read large newspapers. They are frustrated when they do not read much of the information they have purchased.

■ Tightly-edited papers with more rigorously chosen news agenda are more appealing and manageable.

■ Newspapers that contained excellent photo-journalism — particularly from England, Scotland and Australia — were not equal to the winners' standards in other areas.

■ More work must be done on inside pages. Many front pages and section fronts are attractive but the design collapses inside the paper. It is almost impossible, they noted, to design around advertisements placed in pyramid shapes.

■ Improve shoddy production standards such as poor image reproduction and poor quality printing. Newspapers are up against too much beautifully-made competition.

## Be consistent

The key with design is to be **consistent**. Choose a style and stick to it. Adopt a design that is appropriate for the audience and content of your publication and concentrate on getting that right. Remember the KISS principle: Keep it simple, sweetie. That is one of the main messages of this book. Design should communicate a sense of order and precision, and suggest a publication has been planned coherently. Design should aim to ensure people have easy access to content. Excellent writing will often get read no matter how poor the design. But mediocre or ordinary writing needs as much help as it can get. When you have good writing allied with good design, you have a winning product.

# Exercises

1. Obtain copies of broadsheet or tabloid papers in a competing market and compare designs. How do these papers make themselves unique? Discuss what you perceive to be each paper's design policy with a colleague.

2. Select a newspaper whose design you dislike. Redesign the publication, either by cutting it up and reassembling it, or by creating a redesign with desktop publishing software.

3. Create a template for a newspaper front page, using a paper layout or desktop publishing software. Follow the recommended design procedure outlined in the chapter. Allow space for one major picture as a CVI, four stories and a column of NIBs. Select appropriate typography and headline sizes. Print your template and discuss it with a colleague.

# References

*Design*, the journal of the Society for News Design, Summer 2000. Pages 20–32.

Goltz, Gene (1987). 'The eyes have it: Another readership research tool is introduced' in *Presstime*, September 1987, 14–17.

Harrower, Tim (1999). *The Newspaper Designer's Handbook*. Fourth edition. William Brown.

Giles, Vic & Hodgson, F.W. (1996). *Creative Newspaper Design*. London: Heinemann.

# Picture editing for a visual age

## Summary

- Picture shapes and visual theory
- Image 'energy'
- Picture choice and news values
- Cropping, or how to improve images
- The ethics of cropping
- US guidelines on altering photos

**M**OST copy editors and many designers with backgrounds in journalism tend to place a higher value on words rather than pictures. They know about and are comfortable with text but often they are not as visually literate as the people for whom they are designing and editing. In the digital world, editors will increasingly need to know how to choose and edit photographs. That is, they need to take a crash course in visual communication. This chapter progresses from that standpoint.

On smaller papers, the reporter's role has changed to the point that they are expected to take photographs. Given that these reporters also have text backgrounds, their photographs are usually poor. Until reporters with cameras learn more skills, it will be left to the sub to salvage the situation — usually by cropping the image — or finding another picture in the publication's library.

It is not possible to make a silk purse out of a sow's ear, in the sense of making a bad photograph good. But it is possible to make a passable leather purse. An average or even bad photograph can be improved considerably through intelligent cropping and digital manipulation. Most news photographers with analogue cameras use good quality film with a high ASA rating (400 or higher) so when the photograph is cropped and enlarged, the image will still be reasonably clear (though they tend to be grainy or streaky). With modern digital cameras and post-production software it is possible to get close to a

---

Some news managers argue that convergence journalism requires all reporters to be able to get their stories in all media, that format specialization is dead. Others can be found taking an extreme counter-position, calling for self-sufficient news staffs for each separate medium, particularly for multimedia Web versus static print reporting. In evaluating news-gathering tools against this debate, the Advanced Journalism Technology Project (AJTP) developed a 'first-on-scene' newsflow scenario as its criteria. This scenario expects specialist video-, audio- and photo-journalists to continue to be necessary and desirable for assignment to news events where high-end equipment and highest quality content are required. However, the scenario also expects that general-skilled reporters working for a multiple-media news organization should have sufficient technology at their disposal to adequately support the newsroom's multimedia news-gathering needs in cases where reporters are the first or only reporting assets at a news scene. To satisfy the requirements of the first-on-scene scenario, NewsGear includes a 'pro-sumer' digital multimedia recorder from Hitachi. The 'pro-sumer' tag has evolved to identify technology that offers sufficient quality to meet moderate professional standards but ease-of-use features to compensate for nonprofessionals. The M2 MPEG Cam is a hand-sized device [weighing less than 500 grams] that can instantly turn any general reporter into a multimedia reporter, able to bring back broadcast and Web-quality video and audio — or at least able to hold the fort until the cavalry arrives.

Source: Seybold Report on Internet Publishing, February 2000

designer leather purse. The boxed quote at left from Kerry Northrup, technologies editor for Ifra and executive director of Ifra's NewsOps Centre, summarizes the latest thinking.

Newspaper reporters are increasingly being expected to carry digital cameras. The Ifra Advanced Journalism Technology Project has been looking at the next generation of reporting tools. They constitute the News Gear suite of tools. Figure 7.1 shows Hitachi's M2 MPEG camera.

**Figure 7.1 The Hitachi M2 MPEG camera.**
**Photograph courtesy of Hitachi Ltd.**

This chapter will consider the skills of picture editing — that is, how to select and process appropriate images for publication. It proceeds from the basis outlined in the previous chapter that pages should be designed around a centre of visual impact, which is usually a photograph. The key sections to be discussed are:

■ picture shapes

■ image 'energy'

■ picture choice

■ image improvements (cropping)

# Picture shapes and visual theory

The most visually pleasing shape is known as the golden section or ratio. Many books refer to it as the shape that is most pleasing to the human eye, and usually simplify it as 3:5 or 5:3. Actually, just like pi, it is an irrational ratio — 1.61803398:1 — which translates roughly to 5:3 or 3:5. Regardless of the numbers involved, this ratio produces an aesthetically pleasing shape. Architects and designers throughout history have adopted it. The Parthenon and the Acropolis in Athens, Greece, are examples of buildings constructed around the golden section. Designer Phil Nesbitt points out that newspapers would be visually dull if all photographs followed this ratio. He is right, because newspapers generally want action in pictures (other than single-column mug shots). Still, it helps to understand the theory behind the suggestion that specific image shapes can be used to create specific moods. And knowledge of the golden ratio helps when cropping images.

Horizontal photos provide a sense of order, peace and organization. This is why landscape paintings are almost always horizontal — it is rare to find a pastoral scene that is not horizontal. Vertical photos imply strength, power and movement. Next time you read a paper, notice how few horizontal shots are used on the sports pages. Photos that contain oblique lines of force through them (most good sports pictures, for example) provide extra movement and action. Figure 7.2 shows an example from *The Border Mail*, an Australian regional daily.

Most pictures have lines of force. They point the reader's eye in a specific direction. Use direction lines to compel the reader to look at the copy that goes with the picture, or to herd readers around a page. If the photo stands alone, for example, use

**Figure 7.2: This front page of *The Border Mail* shows the powerful lines of force in the main sports photograph. Note the space that could have been cropped at the base of the image.**

Picture courtesy of the Pacific Area Newspaper Publishers' Association.

the lines of force (such as an outstretched arm) to push the reader towards another story or image. If the story you are editing refers to two people in conflict with each other and you include profile images of them, design the page so the images oppose each other to use lines of force. Never allow the lines of force to push readers off a page before they have had a chance to take in as much of the content as possible.

Vertical or horizontal shapes look better than squares. The square is boring. I suppose this explains the 1950s word to describe a conservative or boring person — a square. And remember that the exception defies the rule. A vertical landscape can be very powerful if used in the right place and context. Neat and regular layouts containing photos all the same size do not work. The eye needs variety. If you have more than one picture on a page, ensure you use one large and dominant image and make the others subservient. That is, layouts should be asymmetrical rather than symmetrical. Figure 7.3 presents this concept in diagram form.

## Symmetrical design versus asymmetrical design

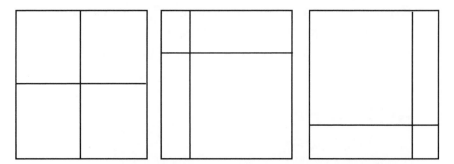

**Figure 7.3: Static or symmetrical design like that shown on the left is boring, compared with the examples of asymmetrical design shown above middle and right. The two asymmetrical designs establish a dominant image and make it a focal point.**

The assistant managing editor for electronic news at the *Chicago Tribune*, Mark Hinojosa, maintains that photojournalism is the business of telling stories. He ran the paper's picture desk before moving to his new position. 'Stories are about people,' he says. For that reason, all news photographs must include people. He urges his photographers to 'take responsibility for the whole frame'. 'Fill the frame. The subject should be more then 50 per cent of the frame. If you don't fill the frame, be able to explain why.' Hinojosa also says that, like a news story, a photograph should contain 'a subject and verb'. By that he means each image should encompass a defined subject, a person, and that person should be doing something. 'Just as in good writing, active verbs are better,' he says. In photojournalism, the best way to achieve action is to remember the lines of force and ensure that pictures contain oblique action lines. If you include people in the image and fill the frame, these action lines are invariably bodies or limbs.

## A few words about cliché images

Too many  newspaper images are visual clichés. Some of the worst offenders include:

- people arranged shoulder to shoulder in meaningless groups with no composition (see Figure 7.4 below)
- group shots with too much space between the people
- the smile-and-shake (grip-and-grin) shot of two or more people presenting a prize or cheque
- the non-shot where nothing seems to be happening such as people outside a building, or an image empty of people

**Figure 7.4: An example of a visual cliché. (In case you ask, it is a group of my colleagues.)**

Photographers need to know how to avoid these kinds of visual clichés. If they do not, editors need to tell them where they are going wrong. And if photographers are doing good things, tell them. A good photojournalist is rare, so encourage them with bylines and regular pats on the back. Many of the faults described earlier occur because the photographer failed to think about the image or rushed the job. Novice photographers, like novice reporters, need to be told what to do. They must also be briefed fully and trained thoroughly.

# Image 'energy'

When Warren Watson was managing editor of the *Portland Press Herald* and *Maine Sunday Telegram* he set out to improve understanding of why some news photographs were more effective than others. He and his staff developed a 'photo energy index' — ways to describe the best images in the newspaper. Watson, now an associate director with the American Press Institute, said the project forced his photo-journalists to find words to describe their work. His staff called effective images 'photos with energy'. For example, a photo with energy 'shows human emotion' or it 'fans the heart'. Watson said that Joe Elbert, assistant managing editor for photography at the *Washington Post*, approached photo energy from a different angle. He separated his paper's photographs into four categories, and these categories are reproduced here with permission and gratitude. They form a hierarchy of image energy. Elbert noted that the right combination of these categories in one image 'translates into an award winner'. Figure 7.5 on the next page shows this hierarchy of image 'energy'.

## Hierarchy of image 'energy'

**Informational**: This is the lowest standard. It is the overall view of a news event. Elbert calls these pictures 'real estate photos'.

**Graphically appealing**: These images are intellectually appealing but do not tap the heart. Composition attempts to carry the situation. This kind of image includes photos with attractive lines and angles.

**Emotionally appealing**: These photos can bare the soul by capturing the right moment — the survivor of a fire looking back at a horrific scene.

**Intimate**: This is the highest form. Elbert said he could not provide a description of an intimate picture 'but you can feel it'.

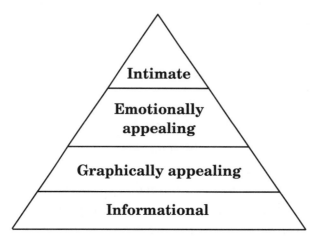

**Figure 7.5: The hierarchy of image 'energy'.**

# Picture choice and news values

The main factor when choosing a picture should always be news values. Before proceeding, it is worth asking what makes an acceptable news photograph, in terms of technical requirements. Editors used to say that these photographs had to be clear (not under- or overexposed) with high contrast, and ideally contain action. And they should not fall into the list of visual clichés discussed earlier. You could argue that image standards have improved significantly in the past decade, and modern software allows us to rescue almost any image.

Photographers rarely stumble on news as it happens. Most so-called 'news' photos are constructed by the photojournalist while attending an event scheduled in the news diary. So the emphasis again should be on communication, education and training. Picture desks need to get into the habit of explaining to photojournalists and reporters what makes a good news photograph. The picture editor or chief of staff must brief each photojournalist when allocating stories. Communication and explanation are vital. A details sheet for each photo should also be provided (see Appendix 2 for an example). Education and training come into play when the individual consistently fails to develop — oops sorry, I meant improve.

Interestingly, tertiary education in photojournalism did not develop in the United States until the late 1960s. Now most journalism programmes there offer photo-journalism degrees. In Australia, only a handful of the 22 journalism programmes teaches photojournalism as a stand-alone subject. Similarly, New Zealand and the UK have a paucity of offerings. In the long term, education is more effective than training. Among other things education teaches the theory of visual communication. Students learn why they compose images as well as how to do so.

Though popular because of its quick-fix nature, training is inadequate in the long run. Photo-journalism teacher Timothy Baker notes that relatively simple cameras introduced in the 1930s saw

Warren Watson of the American Press Institute, Joe Elbert of the *Washington Post* and Karl Kuntz of the *Columbus Dispatch* have compiled a list of questions that editors should keep in mind when looking at pictures. Again, these are reproduced here with permission and gratitude.

1. Does the photo communicate quicker, stronger, better or more eloquently than a simple sentence?
2. Does the photo have visual content, or stop short of elevating the story?
3. Does the photo go beyond the trite or the obvious?
4. Does the photo have enough impact to move the reader?
5. Is the photo mindless documentation?
6. Does the photo communicate effectively? A good photo should move, excite, entertain, inform or help readers understand the story.

a trend of sending any newspaper staff member out with a camera, and introduced the phrase 'f8 and be there'. It meant, said Baker, 'to hell with the technical considerations, just get to the scene and capture the moment' by setting the manual camera's aperture at f8. Technology is so common and so complex that people need an education to see beyond simply how to use the tools, Baker maintains. And a good education will include discussion about ethics because photojournalists work in situations where they need to be prepared, and to have established an ethical foundation before they click the shutter.

## Ethics in the blink of an eye

As Ben Brink writes in the June 1988 edition of *News Photographer*, the magazine of the National Press Photographers' Association in America, it is not possible to do good ethics in a 125th of a second. 'It's doubtful if many photographers have had any training in ethics apart from their job,' he wrote. 'While on-the-job training is good, it is no substitute for thinking about what you believe before you are forced to choose. Most photographers are ethical, but are sometimes forced by editors, or their own egos, to make decisions that are unethical.'

Diary jobs are photographers' staple diet. Speeches, lunches, political gatherings and public relations events can all be relied on to produce photographs. But the results can be unspeakably boring. An intelligent photographer can get a good (occasionally brilliant) picture, if she or he watches for the unusual incident, event or action and thinks about the job. Sometimes what is going on in the background is more interesting than the subject.

Photographers must be told to be enterprising, to look for the unusual angle. And they must be willing to construct their images by getting people to pose. They must not allow themselves to be overawed by an individual's perceived importance. Most people at public events are happy to be moved around if the photographer explains that it will make a better picture. Obviously, the context and situation will influence any decision of what photograph to use. If that fuzzy image in your hands is for the front page and is the only available picture, then you will probably use it.

Interestingly, a really important picture can be blown up to massive size, and any imperfections seem to heighten the drama. Examples include the Kennedy shooting and the *Challenger* space shuttle disaster, and more recently the Concorde with its engine on fire as it took off in Paris. The software supplied with high-end digital cameras can improve images significantly, as can image-enhancement software such as Adobe PhotoShop. A small number of news photographs are snapped on the run. Sometimes the photojournalist shoots on instinct, relying on innate abilities, fast film and a motor drive to get as many shots as possible. In these situations, the image delivered to the editor may need work. In this sense, each image the sub receives should be regarded as raw material. This leads us to the next section, on cropping.

# Cropping, or how to improve images

Images often reach the subs' desk with too much wasted space around the essentials. Or the photographer has produced the best image available, not knowing what shape the picture desk or designer wanted. Or an inexperienced reporter took the photograph because all the photo-journalists were busy on other jobs. Cropping usually improves an image. The golden rule of picture editing has always been: **crop severely and enlarge generously**.

> **Tips from the professionals**
>
> A picture should contain one statement. Crop to that statement. Then position the image for impact — the centre of visual impact, or CVI — and place your text around that CVI. Take responsibility for the whole frame. Mark Hinojosa, assistant managing editor for electronic news at the *Chicago Tribune* and a former photographer, tells his people to crop inside the camera lens and to 'fill the frame'. 'If you don't fill the frame, be able to explain why. If an element does not add information, take it out.' This advice applies equally well to cropping.

Things have not changed much with digital technology. Trim away the surplus until it hurts. Mask the edges of the image on the screen with pieces of paper or your hands and move slowly inwards. It is surprising how far you can go and still make sense.

Detail will print more clearly if you have lots of contrast. Choose your pictures accordingly. If your photographers are still using cameras with film, insist they use film that provides good contrast. The better quality — for that read most expensive — digital cameras provide images with millions of pixels (picture elements) and these mean you can crop and enlarge without losing quality.

# The ethics of cropping

Harmless improvements may be done to pictures, provided you act with care. If an engaged couple are standing too far apart, you might choose to move them together. It is probably acceptable to cut through blank space to bring people closer, or to use digital tools to remove blemishes or unnecessary visual distractions.

But it is vital to distinguish between improvements and faking. Faking is when you show two people together who were never together on the date of the photograph. Or when you superimpose a person so the reader believes something that is not true. Reversing a negative can also be dangerous. Avoid the temptation to turn a photograph the other way because it looks better or fits your needs for line of force. You risk moving a scar from one side of a person's cheek to another, or switching a wedding ring, or altering a person's features (people are not symmetrical: one side of a face can be quite different from the other). Ask yourself, are you being fair and accurate? Never fake, and beware the temptation to reverse a negative.

Ethics becomes a key issue in selecting images. Senior editors choose what will appear on the front page. They decide what the public will see and in so doing present their paper's ethical guidelines or choices to the world. Some people have argued that it is inappropriate to teach ethics — these people believe you cannot set ethical guidelines because ethics, like morals, are personal. This may apply for individuals, but journalism serves the public and is a public process. Selecting images, especially controversial ones for the front page, becomes very much a public issue. Those selections affect many readers. As editor of the *Auckland Star* in New Zealand, Jim Tucker permitted publication on the front page of a row of four sets of gumboots (Wellingtons in the UK, rubber boots in the US and Canada). A man had thrown himself and his children from Auckland's harbour bridge. A photographer and reporter had visited the family's house but no one had answered. So the pair lined up the gumboots on the back step and photographed them. 'As editor I foolishly cleared publication of this across the front page — and paid the price of numerous cancelled subscriptions as readers reacted to such a gross invasion of private grief,' Tucker said.

## Keep it simple

Avoid the temptation to play tricks with images like writing headlines with letters made from pictures or cutting around people's heads to superimpose them on to another photograph. Cut-outs and similar tricks can be time consuming and often detract from the message. Remember the KISS principle. Worse still are pictures that give people unnecessary lobotomies, square heads, or slice off parts of their anatomy. Never crop limbs at the joint — the reader sees a paraplegic. But if you crop between a limb, the reader's mind's eye supplies the missing material. Keep tricks to a minimum. Play it straight and keep it simple.

Avoid the cliché of 'firing squad' groups. If you have no choice, enliven the picture by cutting and merely showing heads and shoulders — that way you get a wide but shallow image, which is unusual and attractive. Always look for unusual ways to crop standard images such as mug shots, especially if you must use them larger than two columns. A single-column picture can be made more interesting by running it smaller than usual, allowing an extra centimetre or two of white space around the image. Or run two mug shots next to each other in the one single column. This single column needs to be a minimum of 10 ems, otherwise your pictures will be too small.

## US guidelines on altering photos

The National Press Photographers' Association in the United States provides guidelines on altering photographs. They suggest that minor changes such as correction of technical defects (for example, dust spots or glitches caused by transmission errors) are acceptable. The association recommends discussion about images that may offend community standards, such as gruesome photographs or images that show overwhelming grief or distress. The association calls for compulsory discussion with photographs that breach community standards, such as nudity, and anything likely to offend any culture. This last scenario is another reason why editors need a thorough understanding of their audience.

---

**Questions to ask when discussing ethics**

Do we have all the necessary information on the photograph? Is anything missing?

What is the photo's news value?

Are there any alternatives?

What is the motivation for publishing?

What are the legal concerns?

Who will be offended?

What are the possible consequences of publishing the photo?

How would you feel if you were in the photo and it appeared in a paper?

Will we be able to justify our actions?

Source: The US National Press Photographers' Association

---

## Exercises

1. Study the main photographs on the front pages of a series of newspapers. Ask yourself if you would have used the im-

ages differently — bigger, smaller, cropped in another way? Discuss your thoughts with a colleague.

2. If you are mainly a text sub, tag along with a photographer on a job. Take a camera and shoot what they shoot. Compare your images with the photographer's. What did you learn?

3. Read chapters in some books on visual theory (see the reading list in the next chapter), or attend lectures on the subject at a university or college. Discuss what you learned with a colleague.

4. Despite being more than a quarter of a century old, the Evans text (see below) is still excellent. Read Chapters 3 and 4. Write a 400-word feature on how Evans's thoughts apply in the context of your newspaper.

5. You send a photographer to cover a major soccer game. The winning goal is scored in the last minute but the photographer missed it. But he did get a shot of another goal being scored earlier in the match. After returning to the office, the photographer watches the television replays. He notes that the goal he photographed was very similar to the final goal. The photographer captions his photo 'the final goal' and tells you the true story. Would you run the photo and how you would describe it?

# References

Brink, Ben (1988). 'Question of ethics' in *News Photographer*. June 1988, pages 21–33.

Evans, Harold (1974). *Editing & Design* (Book Four — *Pictures on a Page*). London: Heinemann.

Kobre, Ken (2000). *Photojournalism: The professionals' approach*. Fourth edition. Oxford: Focal Press.

Northrup, Kerry (2000). 'News trek: The next generation' in *The Seybold Report on Internet Publishing*, February 2000, pages 16–22.

Sellers, Leslie (1972). *The Simple Subs Book*. Oxford: Pergamon Press. See Chapter 10.

Tucker, Jim (1992). *Kiwi Journalist*. Auckland: Longman.

# Using visuals to explain complexity

**8**

## Summary

- Visuals simplify complex detail
- The next generation of readers
- Types of visuals
- Preparing visuals
- Commercial software packages and graphs

**F**OR the purpose of this book, a visual is a term for display elements, apart from photographs. Visuals include graphs, charts, logos, drawings, cartoons and maps. Used appropriately, they are excellent ways to explain complex issues. American journalists coined the term 'information graphic' to describe them, and this has become abbreviated to 'info-graphic'. The national paper *USA Today* and *Time* magazine have become world leaders in their use of visuals, especially 'info-graphics'.

A visual can be anything from a simple arrow through to a complex diagram. Like good writing, the best are easy to understand the first time we encounter them. People comprehend visual detail more quickly than with text or numbers alone. One way to make this point is via examples. Figure 8.1

shows (at left) the way the Australian dollar is performing against the greenback, while the other graphic offers today's weather forecast.

**Figure 8.1: The info-graphic on the left lets readers see the Australian dollar's performance against the greenback. The graphic on the right shows today's weather at a glance.**

Digital technology combined with improved printing means that subs can create info-graphics more easily than in the past. Modern front-end systems allow us to import graphics from agencies such as Associated Press <www.ap.org>, Knight-Ridder Tribune Information Services <www.krtdirect.com> and Australian Associated Press <aap.com.au>, just as we can receive text and photographs from news agencies. And better newsprint and tighter registration permit better reproduction.

The application of graphic design principles at newspapers has probably also made visuals more acceptable. The spread of the Macintosh computer, with its ability to produce info-graphics quickly and easily, was another influential factor. These days, the world's great English-language newspapers such as *The New York Times* and the *Financial Times* display an info-graphic or a diagram on almost every second news page, and more often in the softer news sections.

# Visuals simplify complex detail

This chapter will highlight the importance of visuals as an efficient form of communication. It continues the theme of the dangers of information overload to news organizations. If newspapers are to survive, they must present information in a form that is easy to comprehend at first reading or viewing, and in the most appropriate form. Sometimes clearly written text is the ideal medium. But sometimes a graph or other form of visual will do the job better. On other occasions a package of text and visual might tell the story best.

Designers and sub-editors need continually to keep their readers in mind. In extreme cases a comic format might be the most appropriate if it gets the message across in the clearest and simplest form. If so, then use it. The Writers and Readers Co-operative publishing group in the UK has successfully produced books on complex subjects in an adult picture style. *Marx Made Easy* and *Post-modernism Made Easy* are examples of this concept.

# The next generation of readers

Newspapers must attract and hold the elusive Generations X and Y demographics if the papers are to survive. The people who read serious newspapers tend to be the generation who grew up before television. But they are getting older. If newspapers continue to cater for them alone and ignore the generation that is still in secondary and tertiary education, the papers do so at their peril. At the same time, the older more literate generation must not be forgotten. It is difficult to cater for all groups. But they all have one thing in common — they are almost all time poor.

The best way to satisfy all readers is to explain events in a simple yet dignified style. Never patronize. Never generalize. Never waste the reader's time. Just provide useful information in an easy-to-digest form. Visuals are one effective way to help readers digest quickly and easily. People have become extremely visually aware in the past 20 years. That is an enduring message of this book: The people who read your publication have a lot of competition for their time. Those readers encounter colour TV, computer games, videos, glitzy magazines, billboards, TV advertising, cinema and a vast range of other visual stimuli. Readers will not plough their way through slabs of grey type. They need incentives to keep reading. They need help in understanding the mass of information that surrounds them. Visuals help deal with the scourge of the twenty-first century – information overload.

Writer David Shenk maintains that journalists are even more necessary in an information-glutted world. 'As a skeptical analytical buffer and — now more than ever — as an arbiter of statistical claims, the news media is an indispensable public utility, every bit as vital as our electricity and gas lines. In a world with vastly more information than it can process, journalists are the most important processors we have. They help us filter information without spinning it in the direction of one company or another.' Shenk believes the 'paramount challenge' for the modern journalist is to be more like an electronic librarian. This necessitates a change of skills and values in which 'summarizing existing information is more of a priority than is stumbling on to genuinely new data'.

# Types of visuals

One of a sub's responsibilities is to recognize a story's graphic potential. It is another example of the need to become more visually literate discussed in earlier chapters. This chapter explores the types of visuals or info-graphics that a sub can use. These visuals include:

- graphs and charts
- logos
- drawings
- cartoons
- maps
- diagrams

## Graphs and charts

Graphs and charts are useful for explaining the 'what' of a story. What company's share price is performing best in a particular sector? What proportion of total government spending has been allocated to social welfare compared with defence? What percentage of the rates collection is spent on roads? Like people, graphs come in many shapes and sizes. Line, bar and pie are the best choice for providing information efficiently. They are also relatively easy to create. Pictograms are sometimes useful, but take longer to assemble. Each offers advantages and disadvantages in terms of the ability to provide information in an easy-to-digest form. Apply some simple rules when creating graphs. Keep the text concise, limit each graph to one idea, use strong verbs in text and omit all unnecessary detail. If possible, round off numbers while still remaining accurate. Make the trend or data lines thicker than the axes, and minimize the number and thickness of any grid lines.

## Line graphs

Line graphs are excellent for showing trends. You can put a lot of information into a relatively simple line graph. Use them for displaying any numbers for which you want to show a trend over time, such as rises or falls in sales figures. Keep them simple. Never use more than two or three lines on the graph, and ideally apply colour to differentiate each line. If you run them in black and white, ensure the lines look different even when printed on poor-quality paper. Make sure you include a heading, an explanation of each axis and an explanation of the scales. Figure 8.2 is an example of a line graph.

**ENROLMENT GROWTH 1989–99**

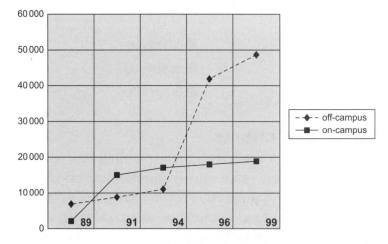

**Figure 8.2: Line graphs show relationships over time. This graph plots the growth of enrolments at a tertiary institution.**

## Bar charts

Bar charts are excellent for providing fairly instant comparisons and are easy for the reader to absorb. Bar charts work best when making comparisons between a relatively few objects. Most spreadsheet and drawing packages allow you to draw them relatively easily, but beware the temptation to go overboard with overlapping or three-dimensional shapes – anything that is not simple and easy to comprehend. Also avoid circles and other odd shapes for the bars — they are distracting and imprecise.

It is best to stick with rectangular columns. Use bar charts to represent and compare quantity via the height or length of the bars. If possible, apply a separate and distinct colour or tone (when printed in black and white) for each bar. Ensure the graph is given a title, an appropriate scale and clear labels for both axes. If you incorporate more than two colours in individual bars, use darker or stronger colours closer to the base and graduate to lighter colours as you move away from the base. Make sure you work from an accurate base. See the later section on choice of axes for more details. Figure 8.3 below shows an example.

## Who do you believe?
### A survey of attitudes to the media.

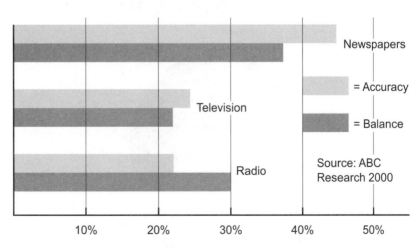

**Figure 8.3: This chart summarizes a lot of information yet remains easy to understand.**

# Pie charts

Pie charts are ideal for showing proportions, such as parts of a whole (slices of the pie), or the distribution of a whole into component parts. They are relatively easy to understand, and the data are easy to interpret. Use pie charts to describe budgets, market share, income sources and expense analysis. For example, Figure 8.4 below offers a snapshot of how a local council spends its budget. Pie charts need a title to explain what they describe plus a description of each segment. They generally do not have axes. Words and numbers should be kept to a minimum.

Remember to use the full circle and avoid distortions, such as the temptation that some software packages offer an elliptical version of the pie. Pie charts need to be thought of as, well, pies. Divide the pie into no more than five or seven slices – any more and the chart gets confusing. If necessary, lump smaller items together and label them as 'miscellaneous' or 'others'. It sometimes helps to isolate a section of the pie to make a specific point. Again, software packages such as Excel allow you to do this easily. Most spreadsheet software will provide a three-dimensional version of bar and pie charts. The results can look good, but because they are three dimensional, the process can sometimes distort information. Use with care.

## COUNCIL'S OPERATING BUDGET 2001–2

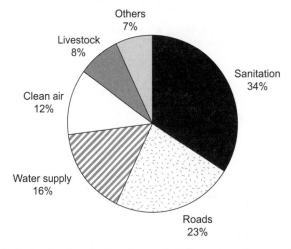

**Figure 8.4: A pie chart showing a fictitious local council budget.**

## Pictographs

Pictographs are best used to create an impression rather than provide detailed information. They are good for showing relationships but you need to choose appropriate pictures; otherwise pictographs simply appear vague. They need a title or heading and an explanation of the symbols or images used. Of all the forms of charts and graphs, pictographs are the least effective way to communicate precise information. Figure 8.5 is an example of a pictograph of butter production.

### BUTTER PRODUCTION IN 2000

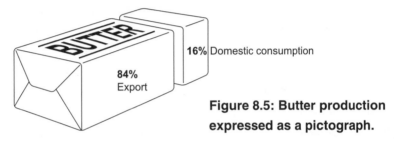

**Figure 8.5: Butter production expressed as a pictograph.**

## Choice of axes or scale

The choice of axes or scale will influence the accuracy of the data in a chart or graph. It is easy to make a rise or decrease look better or worse than it really is by distorting the axes. Always ensure the axes of any graph you create are fair and accurate. Space permitting, start from a consistent point. Generally this means using a zero base. Figure 8.6 shows an example of a dodgy graph because of an inaccurate axis.

### SALES SUCCESS 1997–2000

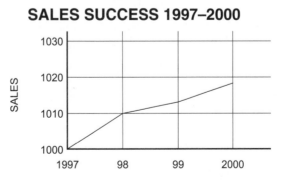

**Figure 8.6: An example of how easy it is to lie by using a misleading axis. Shown from a zero base, the rise is small.**

## Logos

Many corporations and companies employ logos to ensure instant recognition of their product or service. Examples are the black horse of a specific bank, the various logos of petrol companies, the crests of military organizations, the symbols of football teams and the Olympic rings. Logos are visual shorthand. As such, they offer an ideal way to identify specific sections in a newspaper. Perhaps it reminds us unconsciously of a time when literacy was rare when people rallied to the banner of their feudal lord or home village.

The sports pages of some British and American papers use logos to enable readers to locate a particular sport easily. These logos offer the added advantage of removing the need to have the name of the sport in the headline — a bonus with long names like basketball or equestrianism. You can sometimes use a logo in a diagram or story to identify a key company or subject. Figure 8.7 shows a typical logo used during the Gore–Bush presidential race in 2000.

**Figure 8.7: A logo used during the Gore–Bush presidential race.**

## Drawings

Line drawings provide an excellent alternative to photographs. They can be prepared in advance and stored on your server or in your clippings library. They can also be bought from companies that specialize in this type of artwork. Instead of the standard head-and-shoulders mug shot of a politician, why not include a sketch or caricature? Instead of a library picture to illustrate a feature story on young smokers, why not use a drawing? Illustrations are sometimes better than photographs because they remove the possibility of defamation should you accidentally publish an inappropriate picture. Repetition of the same photograph on a series of pages can be boring, but you can repeat a simple drawing several times as a theme. Drawings and illustrations are also useful for linking a magazine feature story that runs over several pages.

**Figure 8.8: Line drawings provide an alternative to photographs. They can be used instead of mug shots.**

## Cartoons

Cartoons attract readers, even if the readers do not like the cartoon or the cartoonist. It is almost impossible to open a page of a newspaper or magazine that has a large, bold cartoon at the top of the page and not look at that cartoon. If you can find a good cartoonist, thank your lucky stars. Treat her or him reverentially. People love to see the famous and the fickle ridiculed. Cartoons provide a fresh approach to a subject. Any sub or copy editor who can also draw cartoons is assured of a job for life.

## Maps

Most people have a pretty poor knowledge of geography outside of their home state or territory. They may know how to find London, Los Angeles, Auckland or Sydney on a map, but probably have no hope of finding Leeds, San Diego, Christchurch or Newcastle unless they lived there or know people from the area. Until the Gulf conflict, many readers could not have named the capital of Iraq. Until the 2000 Olympics, I suspect many people did not know where Sydney was. Maps are becoming increasingly useful for explaining the 'where' of a story. TV has known this fact for years.

You are probably thinking 'When do I have time to arrange a map, given that I need to sub 15 to 20 stories for the first edition in the next few hours. And where do I find the space?' My response is preparation and selection. Obviously not every story needs a map. Consider the relative importance of the story, and whether a map is relevant. If you hear about a news event on the radio on your way to work, and think the event might become a page lead, dig out a map and draw a simple version, incorporating only the key points. It should take but a few minutes and will help you understand the situation more clearly. That rough can be given to an artist. A good artist or graphic designer (especially if she or he has a Macintosh) can prepare a simple map in a few minutes. Software with pre-prepared maps can be bought off the shelf or from agencies. It takes only minutes for a skilled user to modify them. Make sure the map is an appropriate size for the story — certainly it should be no smaller than a single column (about 12–15 ems).

**Figure 8.9: The Sydney Morning Herald includes the 'Ten-Minute Herald' at the back of its first section, in recognition of the fact that busy people have limited time.**

Image courtesy of the Pacific Area Newspaper Publishers' Association.

Ensure that people can absorb any information in the map quickly by limiting the amount of data, and yet still ensure the map is accurate. Get into the habit of accumulating maps. *USA Today* recommends to its staff that every time they take a trip, they bring back a map or guidebook. You can never have too many maps. You can find them at tourist offices, petrol stations and sundry other places. Tourist maps are helpful because they often pinpoint famous landmarks. Car rental organizations are also good sources. Next time you take a flight, says *USA Today*, grab the plane's emergency directions card. The in-flight magazine contains the airline's route and terminal layouts. Keep the pamphlets that tour guides hand out at famous buildings or sites — the pamphlets often contain good sketches along with the maps. With time you will gather a sizeable collection of excellent maps. All can be modified. But the key is forward thinking and preparation.

## Geographical Information Systems

Geographical Information Systems (GIS) offer an exciting development in preparing maps and related visuals. In the US, journalists are using GIS to transform complicated raw data into award-winning stories. See the Martha Stone article in the recommended readings for examples of how newspapers are using GIS. One of the best things about GIS is its ability to allow readers to visualize data. It gives journalists the opportunity to convey trends and patterns. Journalism educator JT 'Tom' Johnson says GIS helps journalists analyse and present any data that have a locational dimension – that is, data such as zip codes, area codes, census data, or latitude and longitude. 'Over time, GIS will be as important as spreadsheets and databases. With spreadsheets you can draw charts and graphs; with GIS you can draw maps, and communicate the results of the analysis to the reader.'

In 1998 the *Philadelphia Inquirer* used GIS to map the city's daily commuter patterns, and then identified the sites of the worst accidents. The same year, the *Omaha World-Herald* used GIS-generated maps to pinpoint areas of high crime in Nebraska. The mapping database incorporated 300,000 crimes over seven years. It would be impossible for a paper's art department to do this sort of thing by hand. Hence Stone's description of GIS as 'maps on steroids'. The Web is a fine source for maps, pictures and logos. But you must deal with copyright issues. See the references section at the end of the chapter for useful URLs. One of the best resources is the home page of ESRI, one of the leaders in GIS <www.esri.com>. Its home page offers access to a host of maps and other visuals.

## Diagrams

Diagrams are best for explaining the 'how' of a story. If a Boeing jet falls off the edge of a runway while preparing for take-off or the local council plans a by-pass through a crowded residential area, you help readers understand the story by supplying a diagram. Some feature stories cry out for these kinds of visuals. A story on how to tie a special knot would be inadequate without a diagram. A long and learned article on the causes of a new disease should have a diagram of how the virus spreads.

The potential is only limited by the available time and the editor's imagination. Again, the Web provides an excellent soure of data and diagrams. See the references at the end of the chapter for more information. In particular, the Martha Stone article in *Editor & Publisher* is a good introduction to maps in a journalism context.

# Preparing visuals

Technology is insufficient for producing good visuals. Detailed info-graphics require research and good journalism. An info-graphic must contain information. Hence the need for journalists to compile the data involved. Here is a simplified procedure for using a visual, reproduced from advice that *USA Today* provides for its staff. First, identify the subject and produce a chronology of events. You will probably use that information when compiling the rough of your diagram. Be specific. If you are reporting an aircraft crash, what sort of jet was involved? How far away was it from a major landmark? Look for place names and details in the copy.

Essentially you need to answer the six basic questions that every journalist is taught: who, what, when, where, how and why. But first, deal with the 'so what' – that is, does the story warrant an info-graphic? Remember the one golden rule of using visuals: keep them simple. Information in the visual must be absorbed at one glance. The *USA Today* guidelines conclude: 'Make sure the designer gets all the resource material they need. They should have access to the reporter, notes, photopraphs, sketches, etc. Don't judge a graphic after it is done. It is too late. It's easy to rewrite a lead on deadline. It may take two hours to redo the graphic. So make sure the graphic designer and the graphics department get accurate information. Get the information to the graphics artist early. Don't wait until the story is written. If you have a graphic idea, share it.'

# Commercial software packages and graphs

Many commercially available software packages allow you to create simple graphs and charts. They are an easy option for providing quick visuals. Excel is a common spreadsheet package. You can create a graph in seconds. Consult the handbook or help section. Many charts and graphs in this chapter were created using Excel.

# Exercises

1. Collect some data series from publicly-available documents such as a council agendas, official statistics or government departments. Examples include budgets, tourism numbers, agriculture output or car production figures. Select the most appropriate form of chart or graph and prepare an info-graphic. You may choose to draw the graph as a 'rough' or use a software package.

2. Find some more data or use the same material from the previous exercise and create another info-graphic. Defend your choice of graph or chart in a discussion with a colleague.

3. Discuss with a colleague the advantages and disadvantages of the various forms of graphs and charts.

4. Read the first three pages of your own or a rival's newspaper. Locate stories that ran as text only and find ways you could have told the story graphically.

# References

Castles, Ian (1992). *Surviving Statistics: A user's guide to the basics.* (Australian Bureau of Statistics 1332.0). See pages 26–34, 'Graphing data'.

ESRI, the Environmental Systems Research Institute <http://www.esri.com>. ESRI is one of the leading providers of GIS software.

Harrower, Tim (1999). *The Newspaper Designer's Handbook.* Fourth edition. William Brown.

Quinn, Stephen (2001). *Newsgathering on the Net.* Second edition. Melbourne: MacMillan.

Stone, Martha (2000). 'Papers all over the maps' in *Editor & Publisher*, 29 May 2000, 22–28.

Tufte, Edward (1983). *The visual display of quantitative information.* Cheshire, Connecticut: Graphics Press.

Tufte, Edward (1990). *Envisioning information.* Cheshire, Connecticut: Graphics Press.

Tufte, Edward (1997).*Visual explanations: images and quantities, evidence and narrative.* Cheshire, Connecticut: Graphics Press.

# Editing text for the Web

## Summary
- The popularity of text online
- Headlines more vital than ever
- Web editing summarized
- Online newspapers: From threat to ally
- Avoid the temptation of shovelware
- Identify unique selling points

**T**HIS final section covers editing and design for the newest medium, the Web. For convenience, the section has been broken into two chapters. Ideally they should be read as one entity because editing and design should serve one function in the new media environment: helping to communicate effectively and easily online. We will begin with important research the Poynter Institute conducted with Stanford University on how people read news sites on the Web. A key finding was, surprise, surprise, that the Web is a different medium compared with print.

Rules or conventions about user behaviour that apply in the print medium do not apply online. A professor of communications at Stanford University in San Francisco, Marion

Lewenstein, has been videotaping readers of Web pages since 1996, noting how they read. In 1998 she and the Poynter Institute for Media Studies used an eye-track device to get more information. Researchers mounted tiny cameras on readers' heads to track where on a computer screen the subjects' eyes stopped to absorb information. 'That tells us what our subjects read. We also could track movement from site to site,' Professor Lewenstein said.

The 67 people in the study looked at only news sites. They surfed to 211 unique news sites and looked at almost 6,000 pages over 40 hours. The total number of eye fixations during the session was just over 608,000. The average time spent at each surfing session was 34 minutes. During that time the people averaged visits to six news sites, which suggests people spend very little time at each site.

Designer Mario Garcia has long maintained that people do not stay long in one place on the Web. This reality should influence design policy. In his book *Redesigning Print for the Web*, Garcia says news designers should assume the typical Web surfer will spend about 20 seconds on a page before deciding to go elsewhere or click on a hyperlink. Details of the Stanford–Poynter study are linked from Poynter's home page <www.poynter.org/eyetrack2000>.

# The popularity of text online

One major discovery was the subjects' preference for text. The researchers considered where people's eyes went when the first screen of online news appeared. 'To text, most likely. Not to photographs or graphics, as you might expect. Instead, briefs or captions get eye fixations first, by and large.' Apparently online readers' eyes then return to the photographs and graphics, but 'sometimes not until they have returned to the first page after clicking away to a full article'. Commentator Steve Outing, writing about the research results, noted that when researchers analysed people's fixations on home pages, they noted that people looked for headlines, news briefs and captions. 'They only looked at photos afterward — and sometimes not until they had gone to another page and then returned to the home page. Then they would fixate on a photo on the page,' Outing said. He also pointed out that the subjects surfed the Web on a high-bandwidth connection, which brought photos on screen quickly. On slow modem connections, text appears before photographs, which further highlights the importance of good text.

The researchers concluded — and this is the essential point for this chapter — that an online provider's first chance to engage the reader is through text. 'Furthermore,' the researchers said, 'the Stanford–Poynter eye tracking study does show a pattern in which text is sought out and either skimmed or read.' These results confirm that people appreciate content differently on a Web site compared with print. Because of the importance and influence of text, this chapter will look at the role of text first.

The Stanford–Poynter study suggests that headlines are even more vital in the world of new media than in the print world. This chapter will consider the important role of headlines and then look at how and why news organizations are trying to integrate online and print content. I will also argue for new content for online sites rather than 'shovelware' — where a paper's editorial content is transferred online without adding new material. This chapter will conclude with a call for even more emphasis on simplicity and ease of navigation because in an information-glutted world these have become even more valuable attributes.

# Headlines more vital than ever

Headlines must be clear and simple. Web design commentator Jakob Nielsen noted that the Poynter–Stanford research confirmed the findings from his various studies of online design that users preferred straightforward headlines rather than cute or funny ones. Online readers are not impressed with puns and other literary works of art. They want information. Nielsen said a surfer's most common behaviour 'is to hunt for information'. Once people have found what they seek they 'dive in more deeply'. For Nielsen, Web content must support both aspects of information access: foraging and deep consumption. In effect then, grabbing each visitor's limited attention is what the game is about on the Web. Garcia similarly concluded: 'Never has the art of headline writing been so important.'

Outing says that in many ways the medium harks back to the days of tabloid journalism 'when competing newspapers barked sensational headlines to get noticed over the competition'. He suggests that news Web sites should consider hiring editors with tabloid experience. 'Of course, that doesn't mean hiring editors who will concoct "Elvis is living on Mars" stories; but someone who's worked for the *New York Post* might have a better grasp at how to grab Web users' attention than someone who's worked at *The New York Times*.'

Nielsen says headlines must be written differently for the Web than for old media. The writing needs to be simple, he says. 'It must tell users what's at the other end of the link with no guesswork required.' It should also avoid sending people on irrelevant chases: 'so no teasers – they may work once or twice to drive up traffic, but in the long run they will make users abandon the site and reduce its credibility'. Garcia maintains that at this point in the Web's evolution, words and writing are more important than images. 'I believe that words are what are going to grab you; words will bring you back,' he says. This is ironic given that the Web is a visual medium.

# Web editing summarized

Editing for the Web can be summarized thus:
- Write effective and simple headlines
- Use short summaries and paragraphs
- Write tightly and simply
- Think globally
- Package material into chunks

# Write simple headlines

Rather than transfer heads from the print edition, work hard on making them simple and easy to understand. Refer to Chapter 3 to review headline writing. For online heads, avoid puns, metaphors and local references. Remember you are writing for a global audience, many of whom have English as a second language, so simplicity aids clarity. Use lower case as much as possible because too many capitals breaks up the reading flow. Avoid visual horrors where the final word of a headline drops on to the next line if it is transferred from the print edition Ideally, keep heads to one line.

# Use short summaries and paragraphs

Because text is difficult to read on screen, and because many readers merely browse online material, aim to summarize stories in a couple of sentences rather than provide all the story. Provide a hypertext link to the full version. Set up each file so it is possible to have a print-only version of each story as well, to cater for the many people who prefer to read their news on paper. If you run a story for longer than two or three sentences, break the story into paragraphs. A good general rule is no more than five or six lines per block of text.

# Write tightly and simply

Apply the basic editing principles outlined in the earlier chapters of this book, such as active voice and powerful verbs. Aim to get your message across as simply as possible. This necessitates a return to the good old-fashioned inverted pyramid form of writing that tells the story in the first three paragraphs. It means writing with verbs and nouns and omitting irrelevant modifiers (unnecessary adjectives and adverbs). It means following the best principles of tabloid writing — short sentences (no more than 20 words) and short words (no more than two syllables). It helps to remember Rudolph Flesch's principle that words of one or two syllables are understood most easily. Broadsheet papers cannot transfer their stories directly to the Web. Stories must be edited. Sentences need to be shortened and a simpler language adopted to ensure stories are easy to absorb. Every word in every sentence must earn its place. Again, avoid metaphors and other literary devices. Think about your global audience.

## Think globally

Edit with international readers in mind. Remember that Web sites have global audiences. Readers in the Australia will know what an 'ambo' is or what it means when someone is on 'compo'. But what about people outside the country? Similarly, the word 'pissed' means angry to an American but to an English person it means something very different. New Zealanders go on holidays to their 'batch' but the word means something else in other countries. A South African has a 'braai' to welcome people to their country but few outside that nation know what the word means (it's their form of barbecue). Aim to use international language.

## Package material into chunks

Think of ways to package material in bite-size pieces. One way to make anything digestible is to break it into chunks or mouthfuls. Remember the story of how to eat an elephant — one mouthful at a time. With online text, break a long list of items into bullet points. Or divide material into columns or use colour to separate text. Make more use of bold to highlight key words. When presenting material online keep it as simple and digestible as possible. English tabloid newspapers provide a useful model for simplifying text material.

## The tyranny of modem speeds

All these considerations particularly apply for people connecting to the Web via modem at relatively slow speeds. Nielsen noted that users do not care why response times are slow. All they know is that the site does not offer good service. 'Slow response times often translate directly into a reduced level of trust and they always cause a loss of traffic as users take their business elsewhere. So invest in a fast server and get a performance expert to review your system architecture and code quality to optimize response times.' This problem will change as technology improves. In turn, faster speeds will directly influence the editor's role as we move into multimedia forms of journalism. The general term for these faster technologies is broadband. It refers to high-speed data services which allow connection to the Internet at speeds fifty to a hundred times faster than a 56K modem (the fastest modem speed available as of late 2000). Broadband allows people to download their email in the blink of an eye. The largest Web pages take only seconds to arrive, rather than minutes.

Various technologies are available to provide broadband services. Two of the main broadband options are Digital Subscriber Line (DSL) and cable modems. The main advantage of DSL over other technologies is the number of other subscribers in an area does not affect speed of service. DSL uses the standard telephone line, which means that in most cases people do not need new cabling or wiring. Broadband technology means that the computer is always connected to the Internet so there is no need to dial in to get connected, removing frustrations such as an engaged signal or line dropout. It also lets people use the telephone while the PC is connected to the Internet, removing the need to pay for an extra telephone line.

# Online newspapers:

# From threat to ally

Many newspapers are overcoming their initial distrust of the Internet and coming to see it as a way to support and market their printed product. In South Africa, the country's national business daily *Business Day* <www.bday.co.za> reported on 1 August 2000 that there had been a 'mind shift' in the late 1990s. The paper's services manager Geoffrey Cohen noted: 'Traditional newspapers used to regard the Internet as a threat that would erode their readership,' he said. 'Then they realized they did not have to worry.'

In Ireland, Gavin O'Reilly of Independent Newspapers also concluded that the Internet was no longer a dangerous adversary. 'It is our ally. The winners in the Internet arena will be traditional publishing companies because of our unique content, inherent editorial skills, distribution capabilities and strong local provenance.'

The group director of research for New York Times Digital, Peter Lenz, told *MediaLife* magazine of 7 August 2000 <www.medialifemagazine.com> that part of some newspapers' strategy was to offer a sampling of the content of the traditional newspaper as a way to add new readers. 'We've found that the Web site drives many new subscriptions,' he said. 'We have 1,100 of the world's best reporters just three blocks away. And a lot of what they are capable of writing never makes it into print. Now they have an immediate distribution channel to get the full story out there.' The magazine reported that the *Times* was embracing the Web rather than fearing it. 'This helps the *Times* move far beyond re-purposed content, which is very important for newspaper sites. Our research, in fact, shows that fully two-thirds of visitors to newspaper sites say they have left the site specifically because of re-purposed content. People don't want to get to the site and see the exact same things they could see in the regular newspaper,' *MediaLife* magazine concluded.

A key to online success seems to be giving readers something more than the print edition, and avoiding the temptation to shovel the print content into the online edition. This makes the editor's role even more important online — someone has to write appropriate headlines and edit material in a simpler form.

# Avoid temptation of shovelware

A seminar organized by the Asian Media Information and Communication (AMIC) Centre in the Philippines in August 2000 looked at why some online newspaper sites succeeded where others failed. AMIC ran the seminar with *Business World*

*Online* magazine. The seminar aimed to identify, by looking at, the Web sites of information providers worldwide, why some succeeded and others failed in attracting hits. *Business World Online* reported that speakers concluded that traditional publications 'must put value-added content on their Web sites' to keep pace with the competition, and not merely reproduce their print content. It gave examples of publications that offered more: 'The *Manila Bulletin* publishes its extensive classified section in a searchable online database; the *South China Morning Post* offers extensive horse racing information; the *Bangkok Post* complements its printed Improving your English with the Bangkok Post programme by offering translation services and vocabulary training over the Net.'

# Identify unique selling points

The Ifra *Trend Report* noted that seminar facilitators concluded that, to launch a successful online presence, 'publishers must start by identifying their goals, content, value-added services, potential partners, the features that distinguish them from competitors, and their sources of revenue' <www.ifra.com>. *MediaLife* magazine published research showing that 87 per cent of online users went online to become better informed. 'The reason people go to any news-related Web site whether it's a TV site or a newspaper site is to get additional insights or perspectives. That's what people are looking for. So what newspapers have to realize and act upon is this idea that the online paper is not a replacement, it's a supplement.' This further suggests that plenty of work will be available for editors.

But editors will need to learn new skills. In a report called *The future of the printed press* written for the European Journalism Centre, Monique van Dusseldorp and colleagues concluded that journalists have to master new multimedia skills to use the online medium effectively. At this point, they noted, few journalists had those skills. 'They [editors] have to learn how to organize stories into structures conducive to interactive reading online. They might need to learn about using audio, video, animations, interactive maps and databases. These narrative techniques and the critical thinking that goes into them appear to be among the most important skills for online journalists to possess.' The report noted that the online publishing model brought some of the forces of commercial television to content publishers: the drive to attract audiences, readers' short attention spans and the need to produce captivating material. 'Quality newspapers, with their established tradition of fair and objective reporting, are at the moment forming a necessary counterweight to the more superficial news reporting brought to us by television,' the report concluded. 'This same quality could be brought to the Internet, from which more and more people will gather their main news intake of the day.

Once online, however, newspapers with their trusted brand names can play much more innovative roles. They can be the focus for public debate; they can guide their readers through the overwhelming mass of information that the Internet offers and they can try to regain their importance among a younger audience.' Newspapers needed to treat their online versions not merely as an experiment 'but as a serious part of their publication's business'.

If words are more important than images in the online world, then subs can consider their future assured. Given that more and more newspapers are going or have gone online, editorial managers may rediscover the need for editors who have skills with words. People who understand grammar, syntax and punctuation, and who have a knowledge of the power of words may survive and flourish. The wordsmith may yet experience a renaissance.

# Exercises

1. Visit three major Web sites, selecting only well-known news organizations such as *The New York Times* On the Web <www.nytimes.com> or the Electronic Telegraph <www.telegraph.

co.uk> or *The Age* Online <www.theage.com.au>. Assess each site for ease of reading and the quality of the text editing. Write a 400-word report on your findings.

2. Compare the editing of the online edition of a newspaper with its print edition. For example, you might compare the Online Age and *The Age* that appears in print each day, or the *The New York Times* On the Web <www.nytimes.com> with the print edition of *The New York Times*. Concentrate on the news, sport and business sections rather than the soft sections, and compare at least three different days. Compare the text editing and the headlines in each form of the publication. Also note any differences in the headlines. How does the online form — the limitations of the computer monitor — influence editing? Write 800 words on your findings.

3. Go to the George Washington University site. It offers links to thousands of online editions of newspapers <gwis2.circ. gwu.edu/~gprice/newscenter.htm >. Compare how online newspapers in different countries report the news, looking at the quality of headlines and text editing. Write 500 words on what you discover.

4. Visit an online newspaper and talk with the editors. Ask them to discuss their work in terms of how they edit the publication. Write a 400-word report on your findings.

# References

Garcia, Mario (1997). *Redesigning Print for the Web*. Hayden Books.

Nielsen, Dr Jakob (1996). 'Top 10 mistakes in Web design' <www.useit.com/alertbox/9605.html> published May 1996.

Nielsen, Dr Jakob (1999). 'Top 10 mistakes revisited three years later' <www.useit.com/alertbox/990502.html> published 2 May 1999.

Nielsen, Dr Jakob (1999). 'Top 10 new mistakes of Web design' <www.useit.com/alertbox/990530.html> published 30 May 1999.

Outing, Steve (2000). 'Eyetrack online news study may surprise you' in Editor & Publisher Online archives <www. editorandpublisher.com> 3 May 2000.

Stanford University (2000). Advanced Eye Interpretation Project <eyetracking.stanford.edu>. See also Eyetools <www.eyetools.com>.

Stanford–Poynter Eyetrack study (2000). <www.poynter.org/eyetrack2000>.

van Dusseldorp, Monique, Scullion, Roisin and Bierhoff, Jan (1999). *The future of the printed press: challenges in a digital world*. Second edition. Produced for the European Journalism Centre, Maastricht <www.ejc.nl>.

# Designing for the Web

## Summary

■ Design for an audience

■ Make navigation easy

■ Design for the screen, not paper

■ Speed is of the essence

■ Designing for the future

LITTLE has been written about designing successful Web sites for news. Most people who design them are probably too busy to put pen to paper. Given the Web's relative youth, it is perhaps too early to draw too many conclusions about what works and what does not. Few online news sites have made money, if we adopt financial success as the term of reference. Success appears to be measured more in the numbers of visitors to the site.

This chapter offers some suggestions for designing useful news Web sites, based on the limited material that has been published and the application of common sense and time-honoured design principles. When designing any product, the key is to design for the people who will use it — the audience. That was the message in the chapter on design for print publications and that message is repeated for Web publications.

# Design for an audience

Dr Jakob Nielsen believes many news sites are not putting enough effort into researching what users want. 'News sites must spend more money on user testing and research in order to provide what it is that users want.' Nielsen suggests that too many news sites are grasping for answers — 'adding a city guide because that's trendy, but not having the research to back up the local-market consumer demand'.

*The New York Times* on the Web is successful because it has a clear picture of who it is pitching at. The editor in chief of New York Times Digital, Rich Meislin, believes he caters for an online audience that is more extended than the one the printed newspaper reaches 'but with similar characteristics: intelligent, well educated, sophisticated, interested and involved in the world'. He and his staff aim to reflect that in the design – 'it's subtle, it endeavors to communicate clearly, and it draws attention where appropriate without shouting'. *The New York Times* on the Web <www.nytimes.com> succeeds because it knows what it is doing. It also makes navigation easy. The publication aims to

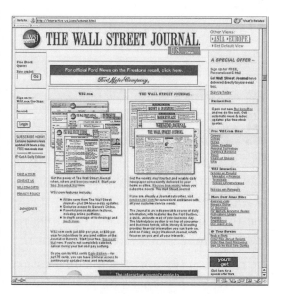

**Figure 10.1: The online edition of** *The Wall Street Journal* **succeeds because it knows its audience, and caters for it.**
Image courtesy the Pacific Area Newspaper Publishers' Association.

ensure that people can find the information they want 'with as few clicks as possible'.

In the April 1999 edition of *Presstime*, the magazine of the Newspaper Association of America, Susan Miller said designers should identify the typical user's priorities. With modern browsers, it is relatively easy to track the most frequently visited categories or types of information. 'Don't make users dig for these nuggets. Locate the things you do best first, followed by those at which you have mere parity with other sources.' In a nutshell, work hard to give your audience the type of information it wants. Make navigation around your site as easy as possible.

# Make navigation easy

The previous chapter discussed the fact that people do not spend long at Web sites. The Stanford–Poynter research, for example, showed that people averaged six minutes at a news site. Designer Mario Garcia pointed out that the typical surfer who finds a site will spend about 20 seconds on a page before deciding to go elsewhere or click on an internal link. Browsers tend to click in and depart if they cannot find what they want.

This means designers must make navigation easy. Maintain a simple design and remove any clutter. Google <www.google.com> and Infind <www.infind.com> are two of the most popular search tools. They have one aim — helping people find information — and their design reflects that aim. Their design is the epitome of clarity and simplicity.

Miller has pointed out that in a time-starved world 'people put a premium on utility and simplicity'. Readers want information, she maintained, not technical dazzle, pointing out that some of the dullest Web sites such as online telephone books rank among the most popular. 'Simplicity wins accolades from highly sophisticated quarters. *PC Magazine*'s choice of the 100 best Web sites of 1999 had an interesting common denominator: Most excel at being easy to use.' *The New York Times* on the Web has adopted a similar approach. Noted Meislin: 'We know our Web readers are impatient and don't have a lot of time to spend, so we try to get people from place to place on the site as simply and efficiently as possible.' For Meislin this becomes a balancing act. 'We've tried to maintain some ability for the design to reflect the ongoing news judgement of *New York Times* journalists, while making sure that people can find the information they want with as few clicks as possible. We're aware that people don't just read a news and information site; they use it. So we've tried to make available the tools that enhance the way people experience our information — instant stock quotes, for example, or search boxes — in a manner that's clear and easy to use.'

## Dealing with information overload

The Internet provides an example of overwhelming information overload. Estimates vary as to the size of the part of the Web that search tools can index but it is safe to say it is growing quickly. In July 1999, Steve Lawrence and Lee Giles published research in *Nature* magazine showing the publicly accessible part of the Web contained about 800 million pages, up from 320 million in December 1997. In February 2000 they estimated the total had reached one billion, and was growing.

A company called BrightPlanet has uncovered what it calls the 'deep' Web and calculates that it might be up to 500 times larger than the known 'surface' Web. In a white paper published on the Web in July 2000, Michael Bergman wrote that much of this 'deep' Web contained quality content. 'There are literally hundreds of billions of highly valuable documents hidden in searchable databases that cannot be retrieved by conventional search engines.'

Because of the Web's huge size, most sites are shouting their wares, trying to attract attention. It is like being in a souk or bazaar, with traders haranguing you in all directions. Web sites copy others' successes and excesses. Too many fall into the trap of employing large graphics and loud background colours because they think they are attractive. Nielsen believes that online sites should resist the tendency to 'crank up the volume' on their pages. A news site's home page should not be seen as a marketing tool, but as a source of quality and reliable information. As Roger Fidler noted in his book *Mediamorphosis: Understanding new media*, the Internet is simply another form of evolving human communication. Radio did not replace newspapers as a source of news; similarly, television did not replace radio. The various media simply evolved into new forms. But people tend to think of new media in terms of old, just as they think of new ideas in terms of earlier concepts (the horseless carriage for the car).

It is tempting to liken a news site's home page to a magazine cover or newspaper front page. But that is wrong. Magazine covers and newspaper front pages are as much about advertising and marketing at the news stand as they are about information. A Web home page should be more concerned with being a source of information. Television was mostly radio with pictures when it started and it took several years before the medium broke free of the old paradigm. It may take a decade before the online news medium defines itself. This partly explains the tendency to dump print content into online editions.

## Employ navigation guides

However, some newspaper concepts do need to be transferred to online products, such as site maps, indexes and navigation guides. Patrick Lynch is design director in the Centre for Advanced Instructional Media (CAIM) at Yale University's School of Medicine. He has produced an excellent site on the fundamentals of Web design <patricklynch.net> that all designers should read. Lynch maintains that the site structure should be visible on every page. 'We take the structure of most information sources for granted. Tables of contents are in the front of books, indexes are in the back. At a glance you can assess a book by its page size and number of pages. Book design is an art that offers a rich variety of aesthetic possibilities, but readers usually find unpredictable "innovations" in a book's editorial structure to be distracting and unhelpful. It is the predictable underlying structure of books that makes a complex organization scheme almost invisible to most readers, allowing the content to dominate the reader's attention. Unfortunately Web sites do not yet share a widely agreed upon structure, and readers of Web sites have long since become used to the dull friction of having to re-orient themselves with every new Web site (sometimes with every new Web page).'

Lynch points out that the computer screen offers few contextual cues to the depth, breadth and context of information offered in other pages of the site. If readers are to understand how information on a page relates to the rest of the Web site, designers must provide that information for them on every page of the site. 'Pages in a well-designed site should share a consistent, predictable design structure, a "blueprint" or design grid that fixes the terminology and location of landmark navigation and editorial links,' he said.

**Figure 10.2: The Web site of the Newspaper Association of America <www.naa.org>. It provides advice to newspapers on how to make the most of the digital environment.**

Image courtesy the Pacific Area Newspaper Publishers' Association.

Miller believes the single biggest challenge people face in navigating a Web site is figuring out what it contains and where to find those items. She suggests employing home pages that are mostly index, or give users a comprehensive vertical index down the left side of the home page. 'This Web site index, or site map, should cover more than the typical front-page newspaper index because a reader searching for an item has physical access to the entire newspaper [while] a Web-site user must view one screen at a time. The *Washington Post*'s home-page index, for example, is both comprehensive and nicely designed <www.washingtonpost.com>.' Miller recommends designing an index so that a click on a category brings up, to the right, a sub-index of all features within that category. 'Nobody complains that a newspaper has too many indexes or that a Web site is too easy to use,' she said.

Web sites I have used for teaching journalism maintain the theme of an index on every screen. One example is the site I use for teaching editing and design <arts.deakin.edu.au/alj317>. Miller also suggests providing a red 'you are here' dot that moves up and down the left-column index as the user navigates the Web site. She also recommends that the names of major subjects or categories should convey the full range of their offerings. 'Use several words divided by slash marks rather than a (one-word) ambiguous term. Some newspaper Web sites bury information about how to subscribe under another heading. "How to subscribe" should be a main header or box, prominently featured at the top of the home page.'

## Hypertext confuses readers

McAdams noted that a problem with hypertext is readers' tendency to get lost, which leads to frustration. People miss the control they have grown accustomed to with conventional printed media. 'Frustrated readers are likely to desert the medium.' McAdams advocates including site maps, plus a table of contents and an index, though she argues that the last two are not always appropriate.

Design principles should also be transferred from the print product, McAdams said. 'Newspaper people must not forget the importance of typography and layout design when they move into electronic information delivery. One of the great things about a broadsheet newspaper is how easy it is for the human eye to scan an entire page in seconds. Although the screen is different from the page, it is still a two-dimensional space. Many of the same [design] rules apply.' This leads us to the issue of designing for the screen.

# Design for the screen, not paper

Designing for Web news sites means designing in terms of 'screens' of information, not pages. Most computer monitors are tiny compared with a broadsheet or tabloid newspaper page. Lynch describes them as 'small windows into a large world'. He argues that most Web pages force people to scroll, but excessive scrolling tends to confuse people. 'Most readers experience Web pages as multiple screens of information. Thus the top of a Web page is more visible than the bottom, because anyone who loads the page is guaranteed to see the top screen full of information, but many readers may not bother to scroll down to see the very bottom of the page [which is off the screen].'

This means editors and designers should provide buttons that allow readers to jump back to the top, especially on long Web pages. The 'page up' and 'page down' buttons on most keyboards are effective navigation devices. Designers should point these and other tips out to readers.

On most browsers, tapping the space bar once is the equivalent of hitting the 'page up' button and shift plus space bar works the other way. McAdams maintains it is foolish to dump the contents of a print edition on to the Web. 'Paper is paper. A screen is something else. Text on a screen is not newsprint, not a magazine, not a book.' Meislin believes the screen is only one challenge in the design process. He noted that it is a lot more difficult to define territories and boundaries (editorial versus advertising, for example) when dealing with a small horizontal space rather than a large vertical one. (This issue probably deserves a chapter of its own.) 'More importantly,' he said, 'it's hard getting HTML to do the things you want visually, not to mention adapting to a variety of people viewing your designs on a wide variety of monitors and platforms and software.'

# Speed is of the essence

People are prepared to wait for information that is vital to their lives. But such information represents a small part of the total on the Web. Garcia and others in the previous chapter pointed out that people sometimes only spend seconds at a site. They will go elsewhere if they are frustrated, so design your site for speed.

Fidler maintains that editors should aim to get text on a screen as soon as possible so users will have something to read while they wait for images to arrive. 'It's one of the things that annoys the hell out of me — waiting while the logo is painted on the screen. Go for what's quick, not what's fancy in design. You can't overestimate how important simplicity is.' Wise words indeed from one of the pioneers of information design. His book *Mediamorphosis* should be on all designers' bookshelves.

One way to improve speed involves providing powerful servers to host pages, to ensure pages load as quickly as possible. Designers should resist the urge to include large images because these slow the delivery of pages. In terms of a file's size, images represent most of the total. The slower the modem that readers have, the smaller the size of the image you should offer. For example, you should employ no image larger than 30 Kb for a low-speed modem (28.8 Kb). Another option is to employ a no-graphics or low-graphics option to increase the speed of delivery of information.

People can turn off images in the preferences menu of their browsers to increase download speeds, so remember to include a text description of all images. Miller noted that a Web site's appearance remains important, but most users get frustrated when a screen takes forever to build because of too many photographs or other visuals. 'People with older equipment often skip the graphics entirely in exchange for quicker information access. At least give users a choice.' Low graphics versions of

Web pages should eliminate time-consuming items such as photographs but make sure you retain information,' Miller said.

# Designing for the future

Publishers are looking at ways to replace costly newsprint with other forms of electronic paper and distribution. Newsprint represents a large and growing portion of publication budgets. *Wired* magazine of August 2000 reported that scientists at Xerox's research site in San Francisco in California, in partnership with 3M, have produced an electronic paper prototype with the contrast and resolution of a printed page.

Meanwhile, E-Inc, a spin-off from the Media Lab at Massachusetts Institute of Technology, has produced a paper-like screen that displays information dynamically. It has attracted investment from American publishing houses. IBM has also launched its eNewspaper, which *Wired* described as the result of a detailed study of how people use their newspapers. One feature that distinguishes the IBM prototype from other solutions is its ability to allow readers to see several stories at once and to enjoy the serendipity of 'bumping into' articles they were not expecting.

These digital pages should move from laboratory to factory to market in a few years. *Wired* noted that no publisher could predict with any certainty whether the next generation of digital publications would look like a personal data assistant (PDA) such as a Palm Pilot, or an e-book (essentially an oversized PDA) or some as-yet-unnamed device.

Lynch has pointed out that effective editorial communication requires the integration of structure and presentation. 'Every medium is unique; one size never "fits all".' He warned of the dangers of trying to divorce 'form' (how a document looks graphically and typographically) in a particular medium from 'content' (the text and illustrations). 'If you need to effectively reach readers on their Palm Pilots, design for that medium.' The world will always need editors and designers, which is a pleasant thought on which to end this book.

# Exercises

1. Visit at least four online newspapers and spend at least ten minutes at each site moving around the site. Write a report of 350–400 words on the ease of navigation, or otherwise, that you encountered and the quality of the editing and design, and how that influenced navigation.

2. Compare the design of a print publication with the design of its online edition. What differences and similarities do you notice? Discuss your findings with a colleague.

3. Consider the use of photographs at an online newspaper. The 'unlimited newshole' of an online site means papers can potentially run more photographs than the print edition. But do they? Visit at least three news sites. If the sites you visit do not use more photographs, reflect in writing why that is the case.

# References

Bergman, Michael (2000). 'The deep Web: Surfacing hidden value', July 2000. Found at BrightPlanet <www.brightplanet.com>.

Fidler, Roger (1997). *Mediamorphosis :Understanding new media*. Thousand Oaks, California: Pine Forge Press.

Kees, Beverly (1996). Fidler is quoted in 'Is that a newspaper in your pocket: Seven experts assess news media in a digital age', a Freedom Forum publication, June 1996, edited by Kees.

Kunkel, Paul (2000). 'Scrap the presses — print and the Web are racing toward the biggest media merger in history' in *Wired* magazine online, Volume 8 (8), August 2000. Found online at <www.wired.com/wired/archive/8.08/epapers_pr.html>.

Lawrence, Steve and Giles, Lee (1999). 'Accessibility of information on the web' in *Nature* magazine, Volume 400, 18 July 1999, 107–9.

Lynch, Patrick (2000). 'Ten fundamentals of Web design' <patricklynch.net>. Lynch is co-author of Yale University's Web design guide <info.med.yale.edu/caim/manual>.

McAdams, Mindy (1994). 'Driving a newspaper on the data highway'. Found at <www.well.com/~mmcadams/online.newspapers.html>.

Meislin, Rich (2000). Personal communications via email, 23 August to 4 September 2000. Meislin is editor in chief of New York Times Digital, publisher of *The New York Times* on the Web.

Miller, Susan (1999). 'Creating winning web sites'. Found at the Newspaper Association of America Web site <www.naa. org/presstime>, April 1999.

Outing, Steve (1998). 'Surprising trends in news Web site design' in Editor & Publisher Online <www.editorand publisher.com>, published 22 June 1998.

Outing, Steve (1999). 'Keep it simple in the age of overload' in Editor & Publisher Online <www.editorand publisher.com>, published 8 December 1999.

# Appendix 1
# The basic parts
# of speech

English has eight parts of speech. Editors need to know them
intimately because they are the tools of your trade. Here is a
primer on these tools.

## 1. Nouns

Nouns name people and things. They come in four types:

■ common (as the name suggests, these name everyday things.
They are generally the words you set in lower case in body
text)

■ proper (these are the names of things such as people, cities
and titles. You capitalize them in body text)

■ abstract (these are intangibles such as love, respect and jus-
tice. You cannot use your senses to appreciate them)

■ collective (these refer to a group of people or things, such as
a school of fish or a herd of elephants)

## 2. Pronouns

Pronouns replace nouns, usually to avoid repetition. They agree
with the nouns they represent in gender and number. They
can be the subject or the object of a sentence (see the next

section for more details). Pronouns come in various forms. They change depending on whether they are the subject or the object. Here are some of the most common:

- personal (these represent people — I, me)
- possessive (denotes ownership — my, mine, your, her, his, its, our, their)
- relative (introduce or connect clauses — who, that, which)
- interrogative (used in asking questions — whose, what)
- indefinite (do not refer to specific people or things, hence the name — anybody, none, each, some, all, both, any, everybody, several)

# 3. Verbs

The third key part of speech is the verb. Verbs express action or a state of being. (For example, in the sentence 'I am alive' the verb 'am' conveys a state of being rather than action.) Verbs are also associated with time, action and person. The time and action element is called **tense**.

English has three basic times (present, past, future) and three basic actions (simple, continuing and completed). Most journalism is written in the simple past tense because of the nature of reportage. By the time a story appears in tomorrow's paper it must have happened in the past.

## Tense

|         | Simple       | Continuing          | Completed            |
|---------|--------------|---------------------|----------------------|
| Present | I see        | I am seeing         | I have seen          |
| Past    | I saw        | I was seeing        | I had seen           |
| Future  | I shall see  | I shall be seeing   | I shall have seen    |

## Person

Grammarians distinguish between the singular and plural forms. Thus we have first, second and third person singular and first, second and third person plural, as shown below:

| Person | First | Second | Third |
|--------|-------|--------|-------|
| Singular | I | thou | he/she |
| Plural | we | you | they |

Thou (second person singular) is considered archaic, and has been replaced by you. Thus, in the case of the verb 'to see', we get the simple present form:

I see

You see

She/he sees

We see

You see

They see

And the simple past version is:

I saw

You saw

She/he saw

We saw

You saw

They saw

# 4. Adjectives

An adjective describes a noun or a pronoun. Think of the 'ad' in adjective as a way of remembering this concept — the adjective 'adds' to the noun. Another way of expressing this idea is to say an adjective modifies a noun or a pronoun. By far the most common adjectives are the definite article (the) and the indefinite articles (a, an).

Other forms are:

- **Demonstrative** adjectives (this, that, these, those) identify a noun (this rat or those apples). When used without a noun, demonstrative adjectives become pronouns. (This is my rat.)
- Possessive adjectives (my, your, our) show ownership (my cheese).

   Most other adjectives are considered as being absolute (for example: final, perfect) or conveying degree. Absolute adjectives should never acquire any baggage because they are complete on their own. It is impossible to describe something as 'very unique' because unique means, well, unique. Similarly, you cannot say something is 'rather perfect' or describe someone as 'somewhat pregnant'. These words are absolute because they stand on their own.

Adjectives of degree can be:

- **positive** (used as a simple description)
- **comparative** (used to compare one with another)
- **superlative** (used to compare one with two or more others)

   Thus you would describe a single body of water as hot or a single problem as difficult. But you would distinguish between two things by using the comparative form. The water then becomes hotter than another body of water; the problem is more difficult than another problem. In the case of three or more things, one of the bodies of water will be hottest and one of the problems will be the most difficult. One of the most common mistakes in newspapers relates to confusion over former, latter and last. If you are referring to two things, use former for the first and latter for the second. But if you refer to more than two things, use last for the final thing.

# 5. Adverbs

An adverb describes or modifies a verb, adjective or another adverb. Again, think of the 'ad' in adverb as a way of remembering this concept — the adverb 'adds' to the other words. Many adverbs end in 'ly'. Here are some examples:

**He sees clearly**

(The adverb 'clearly' describes or modifies the verb 'sees'.)

**He found a newly minted coin**

(The adverb 'newly' describes or modifies the adjective 'minted'.)

**He sees very poorly**

(The adverb 'very' describes or modifies the adverb 'poorly'.)

# 6. Prepositions

A preposition is a linking word — it joins its object with a preceding word or phrase. For example, in the phrase 'a herd of elephants' the object is elephants and the preposition links the phrase by telling us what kind of animals are in the herd. In the sentence 'We are heading to Sydney' the preposition tells where we are heading. Most prepositions are short. Some examples are: of, to, in, on, for, with, by.

# 7. Conjunctions

Conjunctions are also linking or joining words. They link similar parts of speech. Thus they can link adjectives: 'fit and well' or adverbs: 'slowly but surely'. They also link sentences: 'You may come. Or you may go.' and 'You may come or you may go.' The most common conjunctions are: and, but, or, nor, yet, however, if, though, although, either, neither. You need to be able to identify conjunctions because you need to know what they are before you can delete them to improve sentences.

# 8. Interjection

The final part of speech is called an interjection. It is a short exclamation that is outside the main sentence. It often stands alone, as in: 'Alas! Woe is me!' As a general rule, subs should avoid using interjections. Using exclamation points for emphasis is poor form — it is the literary equivalent of digging someone in the ribs to point out the punch line of your joke. It means you cannot write well enough to make your point without them.

# The exceptions from page 29

English can best be described as a language of conventions rather than rules. Hence we have the basic convention that the subject controls the verb. But note these exceptions.

1.  If two subjects are linked by 'either or' or 'neither nor', the verb agrees with the <u>nearer</u> subject.

    Thus: **Neither the news editor nor any of her reporters <u>have</u> received the phone call.**

2.  If one subject is affirmative and the other negative, the verb agrees with the affirmative subject.

    Thus: **The chief sub, not her deputies, <u>was</u> at lunch.**

3.  Nouns that are plural in form but singular in number take a singular verb.

    Thus: **News is what the chief of staff <u>says</u> it is.** Or: **Thirty pages <u>is</u> a lot of copy.**

4.  Singular pronouns such as 'everyone' take a singular verb. None can be either singular or plural, but traditionally it has been regarded as singular because it is a contraction of 'not one'.

    Thus: **Everyone <u>plans</u> to come to the party.**

    And: **None of the women <u>was</u> able to attend the meeting.**

5.  Collective nouns <u>usually</u> take a singular verb. But this depends on your newspaper's house style. Consult the style book.

    Thus: **The team <u>is</u> going to Sydney to play the final.**

# Appendix 2
# Photo data sheet

**PHOTO DATA SHEET**

Date photo taken:

Picture details:

**(Remember to get full names, ages and titles)**

Contact person at venue:

Phone number:

Photographer:

Phone number:

Publication:

Date of delivery:

# Books consulted

Bergman, Michael (2000). 'The deep Web: Surfacing hidden value', July 2000. Found at BrightPlanet <www.bright planet.com>.

Bowles, Dorothy & Borden, Diane (2000). *Creative Editing*. Third edition. Stamford, CT: Wadsworth.

Brink, Ben (1988). 'Question of ethics' in *News Photographer,* June 1988, 21–33.

Buzan, Tony (1972). *Use your head.* London: BBC Books.

Castles, Ian (1992). *Surviving Statistics: A user's guide to the basics.* (Australian Bureau of Statistics 1332.0).

*Design*, the journal of the Society for News Design, Summer 2000.

Evans, Harold (1974). *Editing & Design* (Book Three — *News headlines*). London: Heinemann.

Evans, Harold (1974). *Editing & Design* (Book Four — *Pictures on a Page*). London: Heinemann.

Ewart, Jacqui (1999). 'Design dominates sub-editing' in *Australian Journalism Review*, vol. 21(3), 93–112.

Fidler, Roger (1997). *Mediamorphosis: Understanding new media*. Thousand Oaks, California: Pine Forge Press.

Garcia, Mario (1997). *Redesigning Print for the Web*. Hayden Books.

Gibson, Martin (1979). *Editing in the Electronic Era*. Iowa State University Press.

Giles, Vic & Hodgson, F.W. (1990). *Creative Newspaper Design.* London: Heinemann.

Goltz, Gene (1987). 'The eyes have it: Another readership research tool is introduced' in *Presstime*, September 1987, pages 14–17.

Harrower, Tim (1999). *The Newspaper Designer's Handbook.* Fourth edition. William C. Brown.

Hodgson, F.W. (1993). *Subediting: A handbook of modern newspaper editing and production.* Oxford: Focal Press.

Hodgson, F.W. (1998). *New Subediting: Apple-Mac, Quark Xpress and After.* Oxford: Focal Press.

Hutt, Allen & James, Bob (1989). *Newspaper Design Today.* London: Lund Humphries.

Kaplan, Bruce (2000). *Editing Made Easy: Secrets of the professionals.* Second edition. Sandringham, Victoria.

Kees, Beverly (1996). Fidler is quoted in 'Is that a newspaper in your pocket: Seven experts assess news media in a digital age'. A Freedom Forum publication, June 1996, edited by Kees.

Kobre, Ken (2000). *Photojournalism: The professionals' approach.* Fourth edition. Oxford: Focal Press.

Kunkel, Paul (2000). 'Scrap the presses — print and the Web are racing toward the biggest media merger in history' in *Wired* magazine online, Volume 8(8), August 2000. Found online at <www.wired.com/wired/archive/8.08/epapers_pr.html>.

Lawrence, Steve and Giles, Lee (1999). 'Accessibility of information on the web' in *Nature* magazine, Volume 400, 18 July 1999, 107–109.

Lynch, Patrick (2000). 'Ten fundamentals of Web design' <patricklynch.net>. Lynch is also co-author of Yale University's Web design guide <info.med.yale.edu/caim/manual>.

Mayer, Henry (1968). *The Press in Australia.* Melbourne: Lansdowne Press.

McAdams, Mindy (1994). 'Driving a newspaper on the data highway'. Found at <www.well.com/~mmcadams/online.newspapers.html>.

Miller, Susan (1999). 'Creating winning web sites'. Found at the Newspaper Association of America Web site <www.naa.org/presstime>, April 1999.

Nielsen, Dr Jakob (1996). 'Top 10 mistakes in Web design' <www.useit.com/alertbox/9605.html>, published May 1996.

Nielsen, Dr Jakob (1999). 'Top 10 mistakes revisited three years later' <www.useit.com/alertbox/990502.html>, published 2 May 1999.

Nielsen, Dr Jakob (1999). 'Top 10 new mistakes of Web design' <www.useit.com/alertbox/990530.html>, published 30 May 1999.

Northrup, Kerry (2000). 'News trek: The next generation' in *The Seybold Report on Internet Publishing*, February 2000, pages 16–22.

Orwell, George (1961). 'Politics of the English language' in *Collected Essays*. London: Secker & Warburg.

Outing, Steve (1998). 'Surprising trends in news Web site design' in Editor & Publisher Online <www.editorandpublisher.com>, published 22 June 1998.

Outing, Steve (1999). 'Keep it simple in the age of overload' in Editor & Publisher Online <www.editorandpublisher.com>, published 8 December 1999.

Outing, Steve (2000). 'Eyetrack online news study may surprise you' in Editor & Publisher Online <www.editorandpublisher.com> 3 May 2000.

Paterson, Mike in Tucker, Jim (1992). *Kiwi Journalist: A practical guide to news journalism*. Auckland: Longman Paul.

Quinn, Stephen (1999). *The art of learning*. Geelong: Deakin University Press.

Quinn, Stephen (2001). *Newsgathering on the Net*. Second edition. Melbourne: Macmillan.

Reed, Rosslyn (1999). 'Celebrities and "soft options": Engendering print journalism in the era of hi-tech' in *Australian Journalism Review*, vol. 21(3), 81–92.

Sellers, Leslie (1972). *The Simple Subs Book*. Oxford: Pergamon Press.

Shertzer, Margaret (1986). *The Elements of Grammar.* New York: Macmillan.

Stanford University (2000). Advanced Eye Interpretation Project. Found at <eyetracking.stanford.edu>. See also Eyetools <www.eyetools.com>.

Stanford–Poynter Eyetrack study (2000). <www.poynter.org/eyetrack2000>.

Stone, Martha (2000). 'Papers all over the maps' in *Editor & Publisher*, 29 May 2000, pages 22–28.

Strunk, William and White, E.B. (1979). *The Elements of Style*. Third edition. New York: Macmillan.

Tucker, Jim (1992). *Kiwi Journalist*. Auckland: Longman Paul.

Tufte, Edward (1983). *The visual display of quantitative information*. Cheshire, Connecticut: Graphics Press.

Tufte, Edward (1990). *Envisioning information*. Cheshire, Connecticut: Graphics Press.

Tufte, Edward (1997).*Visual explanations: images and quantities, evidence and narrative*. Cheshire, Connecticut: Graphics Press.

van Dusseldorp, Monique, Scullion, Roisin and Bierhoff, Jan (1999). *The future of the printed press: challenges in a digital world*. Second edition. Produced for the European Journalism Centre, Maastricht <www.ejc.nl>.

Venolia, Jan (1987). *Rewrite Right: How to revise your way to better writing*. San Francisco: Ten Speed Press.

# Glossary of editing terms

**Banner**  headline that covers the full width of the page; usually a major story.

**Basket**  originally, the wire basket on the subs' desks into which finished copy was placed by reporters. The term has been retained in computerized editing systems.

**Block**  old-fashioned term for a picture or illustration.

**Block line**  another name for a **caption** (see also **cutline**).

**Blurb**  front page graphic or story that points to a story inside the paper.

**Body type**  the main text, the type in which stories are set (excluding intros and headlines).

**Bold**  blacker type used for paragraphs a layout sub wants to stand out against other paragraphs.

**Box**  story enclosed by a box of ruled lines (rules).

**Breaking story**  developing story, a saga that continues over several hours.

**Breakout quote**  a quote highlighted in larger text in the body of the story.

**Brief/nib**  (news in brief) one paragraph item, usually used in a column of briefs.

**Broadsheet**  refers to the size of the page. The other common size is the tabloid, half the size of the broadsheet.

**Byline**  reporter's name on a story.

**Caps & lower case**  combination of capitals and lower case in a headline (as opposed to all caps).

**Caps**  capital letters.

**Caption**  English term for the explanatory words beneath an illustration. The American term is **cutline**.

**Check sub**  the editor who revises stories after a sub has worked on them (see **revise sub**).

**Column rule** ruled line that separates columns.

**Column** vertical columns that organize type on a page; from 6 to 10 on a broadsheet page. Can be varied in size in computerized page layouts.

**Comp room** composing room where pages used to be assembled prior to printing. Has disappeared with the arrival of computerized page composition but the term is sometimes still used to refer to the general assembly area.

**Comp** short for compositor — a printer who used to assemble type and page components on a page. On computerized newspapers, journalists do the job on screen.

**Copy** stories and other material to be printed.

**Cut** to remove words from a story.

**Cutline** see **caption**.

**Dateline** For example: 'Hong Kong, Monday'. Place and time where a story was filed.

**Deadline** time when the last copy can be accepted for a page or for the next edition.

**Deck** one line of headline.

**DEI** abbreviation for direct editorial input — the term used to describe journalists putting text and images directly into a computerized editing system.

**Dinkus** small graphic (also known as logo) that labels an article or column.

**Display ads** large adverts (that is, not classified), usually with large headlines and some form of graphic.

**Dummy** a page layout, a sheet of paper ruled up in columns and centimetres or inches on which a sub designs a page. In some countries it also applies to the layout of the whole paper prepared by the advertising department showing where ads and editorial space will fall.

**Ear** space on either side of flag or title. If used for advertising it usually costs more.

**Editorial** a column in which the paper expresses its opinion. Also called the leader. Advertising and production departments use the term for all editorial space in the paper.

**Em, en** printing measurements of horizontal space. Measures column width. An en is half an em.

**Filler** brief story used to fill gaps on a page.

**Flag** alternate name for a title. The newspaper's identity at the top on page 1.

**Fudge** 'stop press' item of late news put on the front or back page.

**Graphic** an illustration — a drawing (usually incorporating graphs) that illustrates a story.

**Gutter** space between columns of text.

**Hard news** straight news based on facts, as distinct from backgrounders, analysis, features and the like.

**Head** abbreviation of headline.

**Index** table of contents, usually on page 1.

**Intro** abbreviation for the first paragraph of a news story.

**Kill** to remove a story before it is printed.

**Layout** alternate term for design of a newspaper or magazine page, though with less artistic or design connotations.

**Lead** main story on a page.

**Leader** another name for the editorial.

**Leading** space between lines of text.

**Live** pages put together with the latest news.

**Logo** see **dinkus.**

**Lower case** not capital letters.

**Make-up** phrase describing the composition of a page.

**Masthead** the name of a newspaper, usually carried over the top of the editorials.

**Modular** design that uses horizontal rectangular shapes in which to place news elements on a page.

**Morgue** newspaper reference library (where pre-written obits are kept).

**Mug shot** photo showing only a person's head and shoulders.

**Newsroom** journalists' office.

**Over matter** copy left out of an edition because of insufficient space.

**Par** abbreviation of paragraph.

**Pix** abbreviation for photographs.

**Point** a measurement of type size.

**Precede** the words some papers use to summarize a page lead. Usually placed below the headline.

**Proof** copy of a story or page for proof-reading and making of corrections.

**Rehash** rewrite.

**Revise sub** see **check sub**.

**Rule** a ruled line used to box or separate text.

**Slug** one or two words used to label a news story. They used to be typed on each page of copy paper.

**Spill** part of a story that continues on another page.

**Spill line** words at end of initial part of story indicating which page the story has 'spilled' to.

**Splash** UK term for the front-page lead.

**Stand-first** introductory paragraph used on features (and some news stories) to summarize the story.

**Stet** a subbing term on copy meaning 'leave it as it was'.

**Stock pic** file mug shot.

**Stone sub** an editor who used to supervise page make-up on the **stone** in the production area. Now called production sub.

**Stone** bench on which pages are made up. In hot-metal days the bench was made of stone to support the lead type and the metal frames that held it.

**Sub** abbreviation for a sub-editor.

**Typo** abbreviation of typographical error.

**VDT** computer terminal into which copy is typed and on which pages are designed.

**Wire service** another name for a news agency, such as Reuters, Australian Associated Press, the (US) Associated Press, the (UK) Press Association.

# About the author

Stephen Quinn is Associate Professor of Journalism at Zayed University in Dubai. He started as a cadet reporter on the *Newcastle Morning Herald* in Australia in 1975. While there he was introduced to sub-editing because it was company policy that all cadets spent time on the subs' table. He later worked as a reporter on the *Central Coast Express* at Gosford and the *Singleton Argus*, both in New South Wales in Australia. At the *Argus*  he was the sole journalist, which meant he had to report and sub his own copy and write all headlines for three editions a week. He moved to Sydney on completing his BA in 1977 and worked as a sub-editor with *The Australian Women's Weekly*, then Australia's premier magazine.

In March 1979 he travelled overland to England. Between June 1979 and the end of 1982 he was a sub-editor with the Press Association in Fleet Street and BBC-TV's teletext service Ceefax in west London. In 1983 he was appointed the founding editor and manager of Television New Zealand's teletext service, Teletext. He returned to London in 1986, where he was a writer and sub-editor with Independent Television News (ITN) from 1986 to 1988, and a public relations consultant and later national public relations manager for the UK subsidiary of Wang in 1988–1989. Stephen joined *The Guardian* in London in 1989 as a sub-editor on the arts desk.

The next year he moved to New Zealand, where he ran two journalism programmes between 1991 and 1995. During that time he maintained his involvement with journalism via training courses and freelance writing. He returned to Australia in 1996 to take up a university teaching position. He received his PhD in 1999 and was a senior lecturer in journalism at Deakin University in Victoria. Dr Quinn has maintained close links with industry by contributing to newspapers and magazines, working as a casual sub-editor and running training courses. He is married with three children, aged 20, 12 and 8.

# Index